MW00711527

Courageous Cooks

Courageous Cooks is a collection of recipes from Friends of the Emory Winship Cancer Institute of Atlanta, Georgia.

This book is dedicated to our Courageous Patients, their Families and Caregivers, and the staff of Emory Winship Cancer Institute who have inspired HOPE in all of us.

Proceeds will benefit projects and programs of the Patient and Family Resource Center at the Emory Winship Cancer Institute.

EMORY

WINSHIP
CANCER
INSTITUTE
Accelerating Discovery.
Accelerating Hope.

A product of type**n**save™ software.

Printed in the U.S.A. by

P.O. Box 2110 • Kearney, NE 68848
800-445-6621 • www.morriscookbooks.com

64809-dn   1

Dear Friend of Emory's Winship Cancer Institute:

Thank you for purchasing Winship's <u>Courageous Cooks</u> Cookbook. This purchase helps Winship's Patient and Family Services develop important programs and services for our patients and their family members.

I am not qualified to write this introduction as a chef, since I have cloned more genes on human Chromosome 18 than I have successfully provided memorable meals for my family. I am qualified, however, to say the recipe for caring for WCI patients with compassion and commitment will never change. This cookbook is about the WCI family, which includes our professionals, patients, and volunteers, sharing another dimension of our lives and commitment to each other. Caring families share, and that is our special ingredient in all these recipes.

The Patient and Family Services Center is designed to provide safe harbor, to be a source of information, and to be the center of myriad services and programs all designed to support patients and their family members through their cancer diagnosis and treatment.

We believe that scientific discovery enables us to treat disease. Compassion, respect, integrity, and a commitment to care enable us to treat our patients. Your purchase of this wonderful collection of recipes enables us to further this important mission. Thank you for your part in helping us "Accelerate Discovery, Accelerate Hope."

Sincerely,
Jonathan W. Simons, MD
Director, Winship Cancer Institute

Thanks to our Friends!

Cookbook Committee:

Stella Kazazian
Helene Rabinowitch
Mary Booth Thomas
Debbie Foster
Sherry Meltz

The Cookbook Committee would like to express their appreciation to the patients, family, friends, staff and volunteers who contributed recipes and ideas to make <u>Courageous Cooks</u> a success.

A special thanks to Elaine Koenig, MPH, Director of Patient and Family Services and Dedra Geter, Administrative Assistant of the Patient and Family Resource Center.

Inspiring affirmations were submitted by Michelle Willis-Styles, RN.

Our most sincere appreciation to Tiffany Barrett, MS, RD, LD, Nutritionist, Emory Winship Cancer Institute, for the time and effort she spent in developing the chapter on cancer related nutrition.

Our heartfelt acknowledgement to the following Senior Honors Students at the Art Institute of Atlanta:

Stela Murat   Tiffany Beard   Susie Fields

These very special and gifted artists created the marvelous graphics for our cookbook.

The spirit of loving volunteerism began in 2003 at Emory Winship Cancer Institute. Since our inception, volunteers have brought LOVE, HOPE and JOY to those heroes challenged with cancer.

Share these positive life experiences and join the volunteer program at Emory Winship Cancer Institute. For more information please call 404-778-2405 or visit www.winshipcancerinstitute.org

Special Donors of Courageous Cooks:

Marlene Altman
Jeanne Anderson
Angel Broadnax
Skip Carey
Nick Demos
Jack Findlan
Debbie Foster
Connie Hart
Elizabeth Anna Iski
Carolyn Johnson
Stella Kazazian
Elaine and Ron Koenig
Ming Lawrence
Sherry Meltz and Friends
Linda Zimmerman

All the Emory Winship Cancer Institute Volunteers and Staffers who participated in the Bake and Craft Sales.

A tribute to the volunteers at Emory Winship Cancer Institute.

Chosen Family

It isn't very often that we get to choose our kin,
The ones who stand beside us, in the thick and in the thin.

The ones who know our challenges for having been there too
And in our darkest moments see some sunshine coming through.

While in our brightest moments, the joy, as well, we share
And have the rapt attention of the ones who <u>really</u> care!

Who sing to those at Christmas time who know the sting of fear
And those who sit beside them who will dry each tender tear.

It's Bunny ears, and Dum-Dum pops, and bears upon the cart
Those things we do to keep the faith of every fearful heart.

It's painting stones with words of hope to those who need them most
And friendly faces, gestures, words at each appointed post.

It's tootsie rolls and candy bars and magazines and such,
That maybe to the folks outside could never mean as much.

It's loving what we're giving, and better, what we get
For every smile we give them, and the one returned when met!

The blessing of each other is the greatest gift we share
As volunteers we paint our souls with tender loving care.

And then we take our love and time to trim our family tree
The one we all have grown with love, this chosen family!

Sherry Meltz, Winship Volunteer

Table of Contents

Appetizers 1-12

Soups, Salads
   & Breads 13-46

Vegetables
   & Side Dishes 47-66

Entrees & Casseroles 67-100

Sweets & Desserts 101-130

This & That (Sauces,
   Beverages, Etc.) 131-140

Eating Well Through
   Cancer 141-146

Index

Appetizers

Helpful Hints

- You won't need sugar with your tea if you drink jasmine tea or any of the lighter-bodied varieties, like Formosa Oolong, which have their own natural sweetness. They are fine for sugarless iced tea, too.

- Calorie-free club soda adds sparkle to iced fruit juices, makes them go further and reduces calories per portion.

- For tea flavoring, dissolve old-fashioned lemon drops or hard mint candy in your tea. They melt quickly and keep the tea brisk!

- Most diets call for 8 ounces of milk and 4 ounces of fruit juice. Check your glassware. Having the exact size glass ensures the correct serving amount.

- Make your own spiced tea or cider. Place orange peels, whole cloves, and cinnamon sticks in a 6-inch square piece of cheesecloth. Gather the corners and tie with a string. Steep in hot cider or tea for 10 minutes or longer if you want a stronger flavor.

- Always chill juices or sodas before adding to beverage recipes.

- To cool your punch, float an ice ring made from the punch rather than using ice cubes. Not only is this more decorative, but it also inhibits melting and diluting.

- Place fresh or dried mint in the bottom of a cup of hot chocolate for a cool and refreshing taste.

- One lemon yields about ¼ cup juice; one orange yields about ⅓ cup juice. This is helpful in making fresh orange juice or lemonade!

- Never boil coffee; it brings out the acid and causes a bitter taste. Store ground coffee in the refrigerator or freezer to keep it fresh.

- Always use COLD water for electric drip coffee makers. Use 1 to 2 tablespoons ground coffee for each cup of water.

- Seeds and nuts, both shelled and unshelled, keep best and longest when stored in the freezer. Unshelled nuts crack more easily when frozen. Nuts and seeds can be used directly from the freezer.

- Cheeses should be served at room temperature, approximately 70°.

- To prevent cheese from sticking to a grater, spray the grater with cooking spray before beginning.

APPETIZERS

BLACK BEAN SALSA

Kay Adams
Original source: The cookbook,"Sweet Home Alabama"

1 15 oz. can black beans
1 cup prepared salsa
¼ cup chopped green onions
¼ cup chopped red bell pepper
 (optional)
1 T. lime juice

1 T. olive oil
½ tsp. minced garlic
¼ tsp. ground cumin
2 T. chopped fresh cilantro
1 avocado, chopped

Makes 16 servings. Rinse and drain the black beans and place in a large bowl. Add the salsa, green onions, bell pepper (if desired), lime juice, olive oil, garlic, cumin, and cilantro; mix well. Chill, covered for 1 hour. Fold in the avocado just before serving. Spoon into serving bowl and serve with tortilla chips. A great tailgate recipe.

BLUE CHEESE DIP

Karen Ketner Fink

7 slices bacon, cooked and
 crumbled
2 cloves minced garlic
(8-oz.) cream cheese, softened

¼ cup half and half
(4-oz.) crumbled Blue Cheese
2 T. chopped green onion

Blend all ingredients together. Place in an oven-proof dish and sprinkle with smoked chopped almonds. Bake at 350° for 15 minutes. Serve with sliced apples or pears.

64809B-05

CINNAMON TORTILLA CRISPS AND FRUIT SALSA

Nikki Elliott

½ cup sugar
1 tsp. cinnamon

¼ cup melted butter
12 7 or 8 inch tortillas

Makes 20 servings. Combine sugar and cinnamon. Brush ¼ cup melted margarine or butter over tortillas. Cut each tortilla into 8 wedges. Spread ⅓ of wedges into a 15 x 10 pan. Bake at 350° for 5 to 10 minutes or until dry and crisp. Repeat with remaining wedges; cool.

Salsa

½ cup freshly chopped fresh pineapple or green sweet pepper
1 T. lime or lemon juice
1 cup finely chopped strawberries

1 med. orange, peeled and finely chopped
2 lg. kiwi fruit, peeled and finely chopped

Stir all ingredients together. Cover and chill for 6 hours. Serve with chips.

CRAB MUFFINS APPETIZER

Mary Kay Howard

¼ lb. butter, softened
1 jar Kraft Old English Cheese, softened
onion or garlic powder to taste

(6-oz.) can crab, drained and rinsed
English Muffins

Combine butter and cheese. Add onion or garlic powder to taste; stir in crab. Spread on English Muffin halves. Cut in quarters and bake at 400° for 6 minutes. Can be frozen. Thaw and bake.

I rejoice in my good health.

64809B-05

DELI APPETIZER

Debbie Foster, Winship Volunteer

1 stick margarine
¼ cup mustard
1 T. poppy seed
½ tsp. Worcestershire sauce
1 sm. loaf party rye

1 lb. salami or ham
1 bottle dill pickles--to slice or
   already sliced
1 lb. Muenster cheese

Makes about 30 appetizers. Preheat oven to 350°. To make paste: combine margarine, mustard, poppy seed and Worcestershire sauce. Spread paste on rye bread. Add salami, Muenster cheese slice, and small slice of dill pickle. Heat in 350° oven until the cheese melts.

FILIPINO EGG ROLLS "LUMPIA"

J.B. Belonio

2 cups thinly sliced carrots
2 cups thinly sliced cabbage
4 cups ground beef (may use
   shrimp or pork)
¼ cup oil
salt and pepper to taste

½ cup chopped onion
¼ cup chopped garlic
5 T. soy sauce or to taste
25 egg roll wrappers
1 egg

Makes 5 servings. Heat oil, sauté onion and garlic; then add meat. Add salt and pepper to taste. Add soy sauce. Cook meat until done (about 15 minutes). Turn off heat, add vegetables. Mix thoroughly and cover pan. Let stand for 5 minutes or until vegetables are ½ cooked. Let cool. Wrap 1 tablespoon of filling per wrapper (see wrapping instructions on package). Seal wrapper with egg whites. Fry egg rolls in batches of 6, until golden brown; drain on paper towels. It's okay to freeze egg rolls until needed. Do not thaw.

Sauce

1 cup sugar
3 cups vinegar
¼ cup sliced carrots

¼ cup red chili pepper
(optional)

Bring vinegar and sugar to a boil. Reduce until it reaches sauce consistency. Then add the carrots and the pepper. Simmer until carrots are done.

64809B-05

FRUIT DIP

Jane Miller, Winship Volunteer

½ cup sugar
2 T. flour
1 cup pineapple juice

1 egg beaten
1 T. butter
1 cup Cool Whip

Makes 8 servings. Combine in pan over medium heat. Stir until smooth and thick. Cool. Fold in 1 cup Cool Whip. Serve cold with fruit.

GOAT CHEESE SPREAD

Mary Booth Thomas, Winship Volunteer
Adapted from "Southern Living" magazine

(8-oz.) cream cheese, softened
(12-oz.) goat cheese, softened
2 cloves garlic, minced

Pesto sauce
Sun-dried tomatoes in olive oil
  (drained and chopped)

Mix cream cheese, goat cheese and garlic until smooth--a food processor works best. Line a mold with plastic wrap (a small casserole dish or plastic refrigerator dish works well). Spread ⅓ of the cheese mixture on the bottom. Add a layer of pesto sauce followed by another layer of cheese, then a layer of tomatoes and the rest of the cheese. Refrigerate over night. Remove from container. Remove plastic wrap. Smooth the top and garnish with sun-dried tomatoes and basil leaves.

HAM ROLLS

Jane Miller, Winship Volunteer

6 6-inch flour tortillas
1 (16-oz.) pkg. fat-free cream
  cheese, softened
⅓ cup fat-free mayonnaise

2 T. green onions, chopped
¼ cup black olives, chopped
(2½-oz.) low fat ham, cooked,
  sliced, pressed thin

Makes 20 servings. Combine cream cheese, mayonnaise, onions and olives. Spread thin layer of mixture on tortilla. Arrange a slice of ham over mixture. Tightly roll up tortilla. Wrap individually in plastic wrap. Place in refrigerator at least 3 hours or overnight. To serve: cut into ¾-inch slices. Garnish with parsley and serve on a decorative platter.

64809B-05

HAM ROLLUPS

Dorothy Ford

1 (8-oz.) pkg. cream cheese
1 T. horseradish
Dash garlic powder

Dash paprika
Ham slices (thin for
  sandwiches)

Makes 8 servings. Mix first 4 ingredients thoroughly. Spread mixture in thin layer evenly over ham slices, lengthwise. Cut into bite-size pieces.

HOLIDAY CHEESE BALL

Debbie Hagood

2 (8-oz.) pkgs. cream cheese at
  room temperature
1 sm. can of crushed pineapple
1/4 cup bell pepper, finely
  chopped

1 T. red onion, finely chopped
1 tsp. seasoning salt
2 cups chopped pecans

After cream cheese reaches room temperature, drain pineapple (discard juice) and mix all ingredients together except for 1/2 cup of the pecans. Form into a ball and roll in remaining pecans. Chill for at least 24 hours.

64809B-05

HOLIDAY QUESADILLAS

Judy Baker
Interpreted from "Good Housekeeping: A Very Merry
Christmas Cookbook 2003"

1 T. vegetable oil
1 lg. onion, finely chopped
1 green pepper, finely chopped
1 red pepper, finely chopped
1 garlic clove, finely chopped
¼ tsp. ground cumin
¼ tsp. salt

2 T. chopped fresh cilantro
12 6 or 7 inch flour tortillas
(6-oz.) Monterey Jack cheese
    with jalapeño chiles, shredded
    (1-½ cups)
cilantro leaves and 1 hot red
    pepper for garnish

Makes 48 wedges. In nonstick 10-inch skillet, heat oil over medium heat. Add onion and peppers; cook, stirring often, for 15 minutes, or until golden and tender. Add garlic, cumin and salt; cook 5 minutes longer, stirring often. Remove skillet from heat; stir in cilantro. Place 6 tortillas on work surface. Spread pepper mixture on tortillas; sprinkle with cheese. Top with remaining tortillas to make 6 quesadillas. If not serving right away, cover and refrigerate assembled quesadillas up to 6 hours. To serve: preheat oven to 450°. Place quesadillas on 2 large cookie sheets and bake 4 minutes per side, or until lightly browned. Transfer quesadillas to cutting board. Cut each into 8 wedges; top each wedge with a cilantro leaf for garnish. Garnish platter with a hot red pepper. Serve immediately.

HOT CRAB DIP

Elaine Koenig

1 (8-oz.) pkg. cream cheese
1 T. milk
1 can crabmeat, flaked
2 T. finely chopped onion

½ to 1 T. horseradish
¼ tsp. salt
2 T. sherry (optional)
⅓ cup toasted almonds

Cream cheese with milk. Add crabmeat and other ingredients. Put in an ovenproof dish and bake at 350° for 20 to 30 minutes, or until hot. Top with almonds. Serve hot on party rye or crackers

64809B-05

HOT SPINACH APPETIZER DIP

Jane Miller, Winship Volunteer
April Leach

**2 pkgs. frozen spinach, thawed
and drained
1 cup mayonnaise**

**1 (8-oz.) can Parmesan cheese
1 (8-oz.) pkg. cream cheese**

Makes 12 servings. Thaw and drain spinach. Mix mayo, ½ Parmesan cheese and cream cheese in bowl. Add spinach. Mix well and put in baking dish. Sprinkle remaining Parmesan cheese on top as desired. Bake at 350° for 30 to 45 minutes until golden brown. Serve with crackers or chips.

JANET'S SAUSAGE STARS

Lisa Sharp

**1 lb. pork sausage (recommend
Jimmy Dean, Sage)
1 cup grated cheddar cheese
1 cup Monterey jack cheese
1 cup prepared ranch dressing**

**1 sm. can sliced black olives
(optional)
1 tsp. ground red pepper (to
taste)
1 pkg. won ton wrappers**

Makes 2 dozen. Preheat oven to 350°. Cook sausage and drain thoroughly. Combine drained sausage with cheeses, olives, dressing and red pepper. Set aside. Lightly grease small muffin tins. Press one won ton wrapper in each cup. Make a star shape--you'll need to fold the wrapper to fit into the small muffin tin. This will make a cup to put the sausage mixture inside. Bake won tons for 5 to 7 minutes (edges should be golden brown). Remove from tins and place on a baking sheet. Fill each won ton with sausage mixture. Bake an additional 5 to 8 minutes until cheese is bubbling. "You can make the sausage mixture and won tons ahead of time and store separately." Assemble the appetizers by putting the mixture inside of won tons and baking.

I experience love wherever I go.

64809B-05

MINIATURE TOMATO SANDWICHES

Carolyn Johnson, Winship Volunteer
Original Source: "Southern Living" magazine

1 baguette
¼ cup mayonnaise
1 (3-oz.) pkg. cream cheese, softened

2 tsp. chopped fresh basil
¼ tsp. salt, divided
¼ tsp. pepper, divided
4 plum tomatoes, sliced

Makes 16 servings. Cut baguette into 16 slices. Stir together mayonnaise, cream cheese, basil, ⅛ teaspoon pepper; cover and chill 8 hours if desired. Spread cheese mixture on baguette slices. Top with tomato and sprinkle with remaining salt and pepper.

ORIENTAL BEEF

Debbie Foster, Winship Volunteer

1 lb. chuck or lean ground beef
1 can bean sprouts, drained
1 can water chestnuts, chopped fine
1 pkg. Lipton mushroom onion soup mix

4 to 5 pkgs. refrigerated crescent rolls or 1 pkg. phyllo dough

Makes 80 appetizers. Brown meat and combine with next three ingredients. Cut each roll in half, making 16 per carton (total of 80). Put 1 teaspoon of meat in each roll and wrap. Optional: brush egg white on top. Cook at 375° for 10 minutes. Cooked appetizers freeze well, if you use crescent rolls.

64809B-05

PIZZA FONDUE

Kathy Fonder

1 onion, chopped fine	1½ tsp. fennel seed
½ lb. ground beef	1½ tsp. oregano
2 T. shortening	¼ tsp. garlic powder
2 (10½-oz.) cans pizza sauce	(10-oz.) cheddar cheese, grated
1 T. cornstarch	(8-oz.) mozzarella cheese, grated

Brown onion and meat in shortening; drain. Reduce heat to medium. Put pizza sauce, cornstarch, oregano and garlic powder in blender on high, until blended. Add half the cheddar cheese and blend until smooth. Repeat with remaining cheddar cheese. Pour into fondue pot. Add fennel seed, mozzarella cheese and hamburger, stirring until cheese is melted. Adjust heat to maintain bubbly consistency to serve the fondue. Use garlic bread cubes or English muffin cubes as dunkers. May serve over toasted muffins as a lunch.

PLAINS SPECIAL CHEESE RING

Rhonda Rose

1 lb. grated sharp cheddar cheese	black pepper
1 cup finely chopped pecans	cayenne pepper
1 cup mayo	strawberry preserves (Smuckers)
1 sm. onion finely grated	Wheat Thins

Makes a huge ring. Mix first 6 ingredients together--you can grate and chop the ingredients in a food processor. Shape into a ring on a platter. Fill middle cavity with preserves. Spread Wheat Thins around the ring.

RASPBERRY/PECAN BAKED BRIE

Jane Miller, Winship Volunteer

1 (8-oz.) Pere Brie	¼ cup red raspberry preserves
1 sheet frozen puff pastry thawed	1 egg beaten
	½ pt. fresh red raspberries

Makes 6 servings. Cut Brie in half horizontally. Spread preserves on half. Sprinkle pecans over preserves. Place other half of Brie on top. Wrap with one sheet of thawed puff pastry. Brush with beaten egg. Bake in 400° oven for 7 minutes or until golden brown. Garnish with fresh red raspberries. Serve with crackers or baguette.

64809B-05

SALMON PARTY LOG

Cathy Hoyle

1 lb. can salmon
(8-oz.) cream cheese, softened
1 T. lemon juice
2 tsp. grated onion
1 tsp. horseradish mustard or
  Dijon mustard

¼ tsp. salt
½ cup chopped nuts
3 T. snipped parsley

Drain and flake salmon. Combine salmon and next 5 ingredients. Mix thoroughly and chill several hours. Combine nuts and parsley. Shape salmon mixture into a log. Roll in nut/parsley mixture or put salami in a bowl and mix in nuts and parsley. Chill well. Serve with different types of crackers.

SHRIMP (OR FRANKS) IN DEVIL SAUCE

Jack Findlan, Winship Volunteer
Original source: "Ursula's Cookbook"

½ cup catsup
½ cup chili sauce
1 (8-oz.) can unsweetened
  crushed pineapple with juice
2 T. currant or apple jelly
2 T. apple cider vinegar

1 T. soy sauce
1 tsp. mustard powder
1 tsp. lemon pepper
¼ tsp. Tabasco (optional)
1 lb. shrimp or frankfurters, cut
  in bite sized pieces

Serves a large party of 10 or more. Combine the first 9 ingredients to make the sauce. Heat sauce. Add shrimp or franks and serve with toothpicks. Good with cubed ham.

SOURDOUGH BREAD DIP

Dorothy Ford

1 (8-oz.) pkg. cream cheese
1 cup sour cream
1 (4-oz.) pkg. chipped beef or
  ham (optional)
¼ chopped green onion

2 T. chopped green pepper
dash Worcestershire sauce
1 8-inch round bread
vegetables, cut up

Makes 12 servings. Cut hole in bread and hollow out--make sure there are no weak spots in sides. Mix first 6 ingredients together thoroughly, then put into the prepared bread bowl. Put top on bread and wrap in foil. Bake in oven at 300° for 1½ hours. Serve warm (not hot) with raw vegetables or crackers.

64809B-05

SPINACH FUDGE

Mary Kay Howard

1 pkg. frozen chopped spinach-
  well drained
1 lb. sharp cheddar cheese,
  grated
1 stick margarine

1 tsp. baking powder
1 tsp. salt
2 eggs
1 cup milk
¼ cup chopped onion

Cook onions in margarine. Add other ingredients and mix well. Spread into 9 x 13 pan. Bake at 350° for 30 to 35 minutes. Cool slightly before cutting into squares. Serve warm or cold.

Recipe Favorites

64809B-05

Recipe Favorites

Soups, Salads & Breads

Helpful Hints

- Fresh lemon juice will remove onion scent from hands.

- To save money, pour all leftover vegetables and water in which they are cooked into a freezer container. When full, add tomato juice and seasoning to create a "free" soup.

- Instant potatoes are a good stew thickener.

- Three large stalks of celery, chopped and added to about two cups of beans (navy, brown, pinto, etc.), will make them easier to digest.

- When cooking vegetables that grow above ground, the rule of thumb is to boil them without a cover.

- A lump of sugar added to water when cooking greens helps vegetables retain their fresh color.

- Never soak vegetables after slicing; they will lose much of their nutritional value.

- Fresh vegetables require little seasoning or cooking. If the vegetable is old, dress it up with sauces or seasoning.

- To cut down on odors when cooking cabbage, cauliflower, etc..., add a little vinegar to the cooking water.

- To avoid tears when cutting onions, try cutting them under cold running water or briefly placing them in the freezer before cutting.

- Perk up soggy lettuce by soaking it in a mixture of lemon juice and cold water.

- Vinegar can remove spots caused by tomatoes. Soak the spot with vinegar and wash as usual.

- Egg shells can be easily removed from hard-boiled eggs if they are quickly rinsed in cold water after they are boiled. Also, add a drop of food coloring to help tell the cooked eggs apart from the raw ones in your refrigerator.

- Keep bean sprouts and jicama fresh and crisp up to five days by submerging them in a container of water, then refrigerating them.

- Your fruit salads will look perfect when you use an egg slicer to make perfect slices of strawberries, kiwis, or bananas.

SOUPS, SALADS & BREADS

SOUPS

BROCCOLI/CHEESE SOUP

Weight Watchers

(32-oz.) chicken broth
lg. head of broccoli
(14-oz.) can diced tomatoes (or
  diced tomatoes with jalapeños
  if preferred)

(7 to 8-oz.) Velveeta cheese

Makes 4 to 6 servings. Place chicken broth in 2 to 4-quart saucepan. Cut broccoli (stems and all) into bite size pieces and add to chicken broth. Add 1 can of diced tomatoes. Bring to a boil and cook for 15 minutes. Turn off heat and add diced Velveeta cheese. Allow to melt. Stir and enjoy!

BUTTERNUT SQUASH SOUP

Joan and Joanna Seger

$\frac{1}{4}$ cup butter
1 cup onions
1 clove garlic
1 tsp. curry powder
$\frac{1}{2}$ tsp. salt

$\frac{1}{4}$ tsp. ground coriander
3 cups chicken broth
2 cups cooked butternut squash
1 cup cream

Makes 4 servings. Melt butter; sauté onion and garlic. Add curry, salt, and coriander. Add broth; boil gently. Add squash and cream, blend-- do not boil. Pour into blender; blend until creamy. Serve hot.

I embrace life and myself with love and understanding.

64809B-05

CHICKEN SOUP

Mike Feigelson

1 stewing chicken (cut up)
carrots with tops
parsnip
1 to 2 chicken bouillon cubes

celery with tops
1 lg. onion (whole)
dill weed (lots!)
salt

In 4 to 6-quarts water, simmer chicken. Skim as foam comes to surface. When clear, add all other ingredients. Simmer all day until meat is tender and falls off the bone. Strain and save carrots. Take chicken off bones and either return to soup or save for other uses. Skim fat off top of soup. Add carrots if desired. Serve with noodles or matzoh balls.

CHICKEN TORTILLA SOUP

Judy Baker
"Taste of Home's: Quick Cooking" November/December 2004

1 cup chopped onion
1 tsp. minced garlic
3 cups chicken broth
1 (14.5-oz.) can Mexican diced
  tomatoes
1/2 tsp. chili powder
1/4 tsp. ground cumin
1 1/2 lbs. boneless/skinless
  chicken breasts, cubed

2 T. cornstarch
1/4 cup cold water
1/4 cup shredded Mexican
  cheese blend
1 T. minced fresh cilantro
tortilla chips, optional

Makes 6 servings. In a large saucepan, combine the first 6 ingredients; bring to a boil. Add chicken. Reduce heat; cover and simmer for 4 to 6 minutes or until chicken is no longer pink. Combine cornstarch and water until smooth; gradually stir into soup. Bring to a boil; cook and stir for 1 minute or until thickened. Top servings with cheese and cilantro. Serve with tortilla chips if desired.

64809B-05

CREAM OF BROCCOLI SOUP

Mary Booth Thomas, Winship Volunteer

1 (12-oz.) pkg. frozen or fresh
  broccoli
3 cans chicken broth
1 lg. onion, quartered

fresh dill (optional)
½ cup heavy cream (substitute
  half and half or milk)

Cook broccoli, onion and dill in chicken broth until soft. Purée in batches. Add cream or milk. Reheat and serve topped with sour cream and fresh chives. For diet version, eliminate cream.

FIESTA SOUP

Mary Booth Thomas, Winship Volunteer

1 can tomatoes and green chiles
  with lime and cilantro
3 cans chicken broth
2 chicken breasts

1 bunch organic green onions
  (available at DeKalb Farmers
  Market)

Mix tomatoes and green chiles with chicken broth. Chop green onions and add to broth. Reserve two for garnish. Add chicken breasts and cook until done. Remove chicken breasts and shred meat, returning it to the pot. Garnish with any of the following: chopped green onions, chopped tomatoes, chopped avocado or crumbled tortilla chips.

FRENCH COUNTRY STEW

Jas. J. Norton

1 chicken, cooked and pulled
  from bone (You can use a deli
  chicken if you're in a hurry)
1 T. oil
1½ cups chopped onion
3 cloves garlic, chopped
4 cups chicken broth (use broth
  from cooked chicken and add
  canned broth to make 4 cups)

1 bag baby spinach, cooked and
  drained
salt and pepper
Italian seasoning
2 cups shredded Monterey Jack
  cheese
2 (15-oz.) cans Great Northern
  Beans (drained and rinsed)

Place 1 tablespoon of oil in large soup pot on medium-low and cook onions and garlic about 5 minutes or less. Add broth and remaining ingredients except cheese. Cook uncovered on medium for 15 minutes. Add cheese, stirring well to incorporate--about 5 minutes. The cheese will thicken the mixture. Gets better as it ages. Freezes well.

64809B-05

HARVEST BISQUE

Carolyn Johnson, Winship Volunteer

2½ or 3 lbs. butternut squash (4 cups cooked)
1 med. onion, chopped
1 T. butter
½ tsp. curry powder
¼ tsp. nutmeg

1 tsp. Worcestershire sauce
1 T. smooth peanut butter
1 qt. chicken broth
½ cup cream or evaporated milk
red peppers to taste

Makes 4 servings. Cook squash in 400° oven in ½-inch of water for about 40 minutes, until soft (microwave for 20 minutes). Sauté onion in butter until limp. Spoon cooked squash from skin and place in blender with all ingredients except cream. Add only enough chicken broth to fill blender. Blend until smooth. Add cream/milk; adjust to taste. Heat to serve.

KIELBASA STEW

Jane Miller, Winship Volunteer

3 green bell peppers, cut up
3 onions, chopped
mushrooms--fresh big pack, cut in chunks
kielbasa sausage, cut in slices

bottle Bull's Eye BBQ Sauce
water (use to thickness or thinness of stew you want)
hot sauce to taste

Makes 6 servings. Simmer all ingredients together until vegetables are tender, sausage is heated, and mixture has consistency of soup.

64809B-05

LIGURIAN MINESTONE

Kathy Cretney
Adaptation from "Saved by Soup", by Judith Barrett

4 tsp. olive oil
2 lg. onions, finely chopped
2 lg. garlic cloves, finely minced
2 med. carrots, finely chopped
2 ribs celery, finely chopped
2 med. potatoes, peeled and
  diced
2 med. zucchini, diced
1 (14.5-oz.) can diced tomatoes
  with juices
8 cups defatted chicken broth or
  vegetable broth
½ cup small macaroni (tubetti
  or ditalini)

1 (15½-oz.) can cannellini beans
  (or white Northern), rinsed and
  drained
8 cups packed, thoroughly
  rinsed, and roughly chopped
  fresh spinach leaves (10-oz.)
fresh basil
salt and freshly ground black
  pepper
Fresh grated Parmigiano-
  Reggiano cheese

Makes 12 servings. Heat oil in an 8-quart stockpot over medium-high heat. Add chopped onion, garlic, carrots and celery. Cook until they begin to soften, then add the potatoes and zucchini; stir well. Stir in the tomatoes and broth. Turn the heat to high and bring to a boil. Reduce the heat to medium-low, partially cover the pot and simmer--stirring occasionally for 30 minutes. Add the macaroni and beans; stir frequently until the macaroni is tender--about 10 minutes. Add the spinach and basil, stir well to combine and cook 5 minutes longer. Season with salt and pepper to taste. Serve with the cheese on top, if desired.

My passion for life creates the best for myself and others.

64809B-05

MEDITERRANEAN SEAFOOD STEW

Suzan Rhodes

1 to 2 lbs. of your favorite fish or shellfish
4 T. olive oil
3 to 4 lg. cloves of garlic
1 lg. or 2 sm. red and green bell peppers
1 lg. onion
1 lg. can of tomatoes with juice (chopped or whole)
1 lg. can whole or minced clams with juice
1 cup white wine (dry)
1 sm. bunch fresh or 1 T. oregano
1 sm. bunch fresh or 1 T. dried thyme

Makes 6 to 8 servings. Chop peppers and onion into medium sized pieces. Crush and chop garlic. Sauté peppers, onions and garlic in olive oil until onions start to become clear and peppers are slightly tender. Add tomatoes with juice, clams with juice and seafood. Sauté until seafood is almost completely cooked. Add wine and fresh or dried herbs and bring to a low boil. Turn off and let sit for about 5 minutes so flavors all meld. Serve over rice, pasta or by itself in a bowl with hot crusty French bread. Goes well with a Pinot Grigio, Sauvingnon Blanc or Merlot.

MUGSY'S HOT AND SOUR SOUP

Mugsy Schwab

1/4 lb. pork
1/2 tsp. cornstarch
1/4 tsp. salt
1/2 tsp. soy sauce
6 shitake mushrooms, sliced thin
(4-oz.) firm tofu sliced in 1/4-inch strips
4 cups chicken broth
3 T. vinegar
1 T. soy sauce
2 T. cornstarch
2 T. water
1/4 tsp. white pepper
2 T. chopped green onions
2 tsp. Chinese red chili sauce
1/2 tsp. sesame oil

Slice pork in thin strips. Mix cornstarch, salt and soy sauce; pour over pork. Mix well; refrigerate until later. Bring chicken broth to a boil; add vinegar and soy sauce. Once boiling, add mushrooms, tofu and pork. Lightly boil for 5 minutes. Mix the cornstarch, water and white pepper together. Add to soup; keep at a light boil. Add green onions, Chinese red chili sauce and sesame oil to soup; lightly boil for 3 to 5 minutes. Serve hot.

64809B-05

POOR MAN'S VEGGIE SOUP

Caryn Shulman

1 lb. lean ground beef
1 pkg. frozen mixed vegetables
1 pkg. frozen green vegetables
3 potatoes, quartered
8 cups water
1½ T. sugar
2 cans low sodium beef broth

1 can puréed tomatoes
1 can whole tomatoes
½ cup barley
salt and pepper to taste
1 lg. onion chopped
2 stalks celery chopped
½ head cabbage shredded

Brown meat and onions together. Drain well. Add remaining ingredients. Simmer covered for 2½ hours. Serve with French bread.

POTATO BACON CHOWDER

Joan and Joanna Seger

8 to 10 slices fried bacon
1 cup chopped onion
2 cups cubed potatoes
1 cup water
1 can cream of mushroom soup

1 cup sour cream
1¾ cups milk
½ tsp. salt
2 T. parsley

Makes 4 servings. Sauté onion in bacon drippings. Pour off fat. Add potatoes and water. Bring to a boil. Cover; simmer 10 to 15 minutes. Stir in soup and sour cream. Add milk, salt and pepper, and parsley. Heat through. Do not boil.

SAUSAGE BEAN CHOWDER

Claire Smith

1 lb. sausage (turkey or pork), browned, drained
2 cans red kidney beans, drained, rinsed
1 (13-oz.) can diced tomatoes with juice
1½ qt. water
1 lg. onion, chopped

1 bay leaf
1½ tsp. seasoned salt
½ tsp. garlic powder
black pepper to taste
½ tsp. thyme
3 cups red potatoes cut in chunks

In a large pot add sausage, kidney beans, tomatoes, water, onion, bay leaf, seasoned salt, garlic powder, black pepper and thyme. Simmer 1 hour. Add potatoes. Cook 30 minutes longer. Remove bay leaf and serve.

64809B-05

SAUSAGE CORN CHOWDER

Donna Wells

1 lb. sausage
1 chopped onion
3 lg. red potatoes, cubed and
  cooked
½ cup water

1 tsp. bouquet garni or basil
1 can whole kernel corn
1 can cream corn
1 can evaporated milk

Makes 6 to 8 servings. Cook sausage; add onions. Add all ingredients except the milk. Simmer in crock pot for as long as you like. Do not boil once you add the milk. Fantastic dish for crowds. Fantastic with cornbread.

SAVORY BEEF AND VEGETABLE STEW

Dorothy Ford

6 T. oil
3 lb. beef stew meat
1 cup chopped onion
1 cup chopped green pepper
1 cup sliced celery
2 T. finely chopped parsley
1 bay leaf
3 sm. potatoes, cut into chunks
6 med. carrots
¼ tsp. dried thyme

1 T. flour
1 clove garlic
1 (8-oz.) can tomato sauce
2 vegetable bouillon cubes
1 cup red wine (can use apple
  or grape juice)
½ T. (or less) salt
¼ tsp. pepper
1 lg. tomato, cut into wedges
  (optional)

Makes 6 servings. Brown beef thoroughly in oil, remove from pan. Sauté onion, peppers, and celery until tender (about 8 minutes), return beef to pan. Add parsley, garlic, tomato sauce, wine, bouillon, salt, pepper, thyme, bay leaf and 2 cups water. Bring to a boil. Reduce heat and simmer covered for 1½ hours. Add vegetables and simmer covered for 1 hour, or until tender. Remove from heat and skim off any fat. Mix flour with 2 tablespoons cold water and stir into beef mixture. Arrange tomato wedges, skin side up, on top (you don't necessarily have to use these). Simmer covered for 10 minutes, until slightly thickened.

64809B-05

UNBELIEVABLE BEEF BARLEY SOUP

Linda Appleton
Original source: "Desperation Dinners"

1 lb. (frozen) extra lean ground beef
1 tsp. vegetable oil
1 lg. onion chopped
1 (8-oz.) pkg. sliced mushrooms
1 (14.5-oz.) can fat-free chicken broth
1¾ cups water
1 cup quick cooking barley
1 tsp. bottled minced garlic
2 tsp. Worcestershire sauce
¼ tsp. dried thyme
1 env. demi-glace mix or au jus mix (see note)
1 cup shredded carrots
black pepper to taste

If the beef is frozen, place it in a microwavable plate and microwave uncovered on high for 3 minutes to begin defrosting. Heat the oil on medium heat in a 4½-quart Dutch oven or soup pot. Peel and coarsely chop the onion, adding it to the pot as you chop. Add the beef and raise the heat to high. Stir from time to time. Coarsely chop the mushrooms, adding them to the pot as you chop. Cook for 2 minutes, stirring constantly to begin breaking up the beef. Remove any visible fat from broth. Add broth, water and barley. Cover the pot; bring to a boil. Add garlic, Worcestershire sauce and thyme, keeping the pot covered as much as possible. When the soup comes to a rolling boil, keep if from boiling over (if necessary) by reducing the heat to medium-high or cracking the pot lid. Add the demi-glace and stir until it dissolves. Boil for 5 minutes. Chop the shredded carrots into bite-size lengths and set them aside. When broth has boiled 5 minutes, add the carrots and re-cover the pot. Continue to boil 5 more minutes or until the barley is tender. Season with pepper to taste. Serve at once.

Note: You'll find demi-glace (also called demi-glaze) mix with the dry pasta sauce and packaged soup mixes, or with the spices. The most commonly available brand is Knorr Classic Sauces Demi-Glace. If it is unavailable, au jus mix can be substituted.

Today, I am grateful for each moment.

64809B-05

YUMMY POTATO SOUP

Elizabeth Evans

2 lg. potatoes (baked)
1 lg. onion (chopped)
2 cans cream of chicken soup
1 can evaporated milk

6 to 7 bacon slices
¼ tsp. season salt
¼ tsp. pepper
grated cheese

Dice large baked potatoes with skin on. Sauté chopped onion in 2 tablespoons of oil. Add 3 slices of bacon cut into smaller pieces and sauté with onion. Add evaporated milk and soup. Add 1 to 1½ soup cans of regular milk. Add salt and pepper. Cook on low about 20 minutes. Add potatoes last. Garnish with cheese and bacon.

SALADS

ANTIPASTO SALAD

Claire Smith

1 (16-oz.) pkg. rotini pasta
1 (15-oz.) can garbanzo beans, rinsed, drained
1 pkg. sliced pepperoni, halved
1 can black olives, sliced
½ cup sweet red pepper, diced
½ cup green pepper, diced
8 med. fresh mushrooms, sliced
2 garlic cloves, minced or 2 tsp. garlic powder

2 T. fresh basil or 2 tsp. dried basil
2 tsp. salt
½ tsp. dried oregano
½ tsp. pepper
¼ tsp. cayenne pepper, optional
1 cup olive oil
⅔ cup lemon juice

Cook pasta according to directions. Place cooked pasta in a large bowl. Add beans, pepperoni, olives, peppers, mushrooms and cayenne pepper. Mix oil and lemon juice; add seasonings. Pour over pasta.

64809B-05

BROCCOLI BACON SALAD

Jane Miller, Winship Volunteer

½ to ⅔ cup sunflower seeds or
  sliced toasted almonds
4 cups broccoli florets
1 cup green grapes, halved (or
  use all red grapes)
1 cup red grapes, halved

1 cup chopped celery
¼ cup chopped green onion
½ lb. bacon, fried crisp
1 cup mayonnaise
⅓ cup sugar
2 T. vinegar

Makes 8 servings. Cook bacon until crisp. Let cool; crumble. In a large bowl, combine first six ingredients. In another bowl, combine mayonnaise, sugar, vinegar, and crumbled bacon. Add to broccoli mixture, toss to coat. Cover and chill at least 4 hours or overnight.

BROCCOLI SLAW

Julie Whitehead, Winship Volunteer

(16-oz.) broccoli slaw or (16-oz.)
  shredded cabbage
2 pkgs. chicken ramen noodles

¼ cup toasted slivered almonds
  or ¼ cup toasted sunflower
  seeds

In a large bowl, toss slaw, almonds and crumbled ramen noodles. Set aside. Make close to serving time, as the ramen noodles lose their crispness if done too far in advance.

Dressing

⅓ cup vegetable oil
3 T. sugar
5 T. red wine vinegar

3 drops sesame oil
2 pkgs. chicken seasoning from
  the ramen noodles

Whisk together oil, sugar, ramen noodle seasoning, vinegar, and sesame seed oil. Pour dressing over slaw and toss well.

64809B-05

CAESAR SLAW

Mary Booth Thomas, Winship Volunteer

2 bags angel hair shredded
  cabbage
2 bunches organic green
  onions, chopped
½ cup grated Romano-Pecorino
  or Parmesan cheese

1 cup mayonnaise
⅓ cup fresh lemon juice
10 anchovy filets, finely
  chopped
3 garlic cloves, minced

Mix mayonnaise, lemon juice, anchovy filets and garlic and stir until blended to make dressing. Mix shredded cabbage and green onions in a large bowl. Add mayonnaise and mix well. Refrigerate. Add cheese before serving and mix.

CARROT SALAD

Dorothy Ford

2 pkgs. carrots, sliced thin
1 can tomato soup
1 green pepper, chopped
1 med. onion, chopped
¾ cup sugar
½ cup vegetable oil
¼ cup apple cider vinegar

1 tsp. dried basil
1 tsp. Worcestershire sauce
1 tsp. salt
1 tsp. dried mustard
1 tsp. celery seed
dash pepper

Makes 6 servings. Cook carrots until tender, but not mushy. Drain and cool. Mix the rest of the ingredients until well combined. Pour over carrots in serving bowl. Refrigerate for at least 2 hours; best if overnight.

CHICKEN SALAD

Kathy Fonder

½ cup celery, diced
½ cup onion, diced
1 cup cooked chicken breast,
  diced

½ cup shredded carrots
mayo to taste

Mix above ingredients together. Add mayo to taste. Chill. Add 1 can of shoestring potatoes just before serving.

64809B-05

COBB LANE CHICKEN SALAD

Mary Booth Thomas, Winship Volunteer

4 skinless chicken breasts
  (bone in)
seasoned salt
3 stalks celery, chopped fine
3 sm. apples, peeled and
  chopped fine

1 cup mayonnaise
½ cup toasted almonds,
  chopped fine

Boil the chicken breasts in water seasoned with the salt. Cool. Shred chicken into large bowl. Add other ingredients and mix well. Refrigerate at least 4 hours before serving to allow flavors to blend.

CURRIED CHICKEN AND RICE SALAD

Pat Liebmann, Winship Volunteer

¾ cups plus 2 T. olive oil
1 lg. onion
2 tsp. curry powder
2 boneless/skinless chicken
  breast halves, cut crosswise
  into ½ inch-wide strips
4 cups cooked long-grain rice
  (white, cooled)
1 (10-oz.) pkg. frozen petite
  peas, thawed

1 (17-oz.) jar roasted red
  peppers, chopped
½ cup golden raisins or dried
  currants
¼ cup chopped fresh cilantro
¼ cup white wine vinegar
2 tsp. ground cumin

Makes 4 to 6 servings. Heat 2 tablespoons of oil in heavy large skillet over medium heat. Add onion and curry powder and sauté 6 minutes. Add chicken and sauté until cooked through--about 4 minutes. Transfer to large bowl and cool. Mix in rice, peas, peppers, raisins, and cilantro. Whisk remaining ¾ cup oil, vinegar, and cumin in small bowl to blend. Add enough dressing to salad to season to taste; toss well. Cover and refrigerate. Bring to room temperature before serving. A wonderful dish for large buffet gatherings. Can be prepared 1 day prior to serving.

My strengths are my blessings to the world.

64809B-05

GERMAN POTATO SALAD

Debbie Hagood

3 lbs. red potatoes, cooked
   whole with skin on
3 to 4 hard-cooked eggs, peeled
   and sliced
5 raw eggs
¾ cup diced onions

¾ cup diced celery
¾ cup diced green pepper
½ to 1 lb. bacon
1 cup sugar
1 cup cider vinegar
salt and pepper to taste

Peel or don't peel potatoes according to taste. Mix well with chopped vegetables. Fry bacon in skillet until crisp. Remove strips and crumble into potatoes. In a bowl, beat 5 raw eggs. Add sugar and vinegar; mix well. Pour into skillet with bacon grease and cook over medium heat until mixture thickens and boils. Pour over potatoes and mix well. Mix in and garnish with hard-cooked eggs.

GREEN-&-GOLD SALAD WITH FRESH CITRUS RANCH DRESSING

Linda Zimmerman, Winship Volunteer
Interpreted from "Southern Living" magazine

3 cups chopped fresh broccoli
1½ cups diced mango
1 lg. navel orange, sectioned
   and chopped

½ cup pecans, toasted
1 (6-oz.) pkg. fresh baby
   spinach

Makes 6 to 8 servings. Combine first 5 ingredients in a large bowl. Toss with Fresh Citrus Ranch Dressing.

Fresh Citrus Ranch Dressing

¾ cup Buttermilk Ranch
   Dressing

2 tsp. grated orange rind
3 T. fresh orange juice

Makes about 1 cup. Whisk together all ingredients. Cover and chill until ready to serve.

64809B-05

HOT CHICKEN SALAD

Julie Whitehead, Winship Volunteer

4 cups boiled chicken, chopped
2 T. lemon juice
¾ cup mayonnaise
1 tsp. salt
2 cups grated cheese

4 hard-boiled eggs, sliced
¾ cup cream of chicken soup
1 tsp. onion, finely chopped
⅔ cup almonds, chopped

Makes 12 servings. Combine all ingredients except cheese, potato chips, and almonds. Place mixture in large baking dish and let stand overnight. Bake at 400° for 10 minutes, then top with cheese, potato chips and almonds, and bake for 15 more minutes. For easy clean up, spray baking dish with cooking spray.

MACARONI SALAD

Jane Miller, Winship Volunteer

8 cups macaroni (8-oz. uncooked)
8 fresh tomatoes, diced
2 cups grated sharp cheddar cheese
2 cups mayonnaise

1 cup black olives, halved (can use green olives)
2 cups onions, diced
2 tsp. garlic powder
1 tsp. cayenne pepper, or to taste

Makes 24 servings. Cook macaroni; rinse in cold water until cooled. Add other ingredients and mix. Great with BBQ!

64809B-05

MANDARIN SALAD

Karin Brown

¼ cup sliced almonds
1 T. plus 1 tsp. sugar
¼ head lettuce, torn into bite-size pieces
¼ bunch romaine lettuce, torn into bite-size pieces

2 med. stalks celery, chopped
2 green onions, thinly sliced
1 (11-oz.) can mandarin oranges, drained

Makes 6 servings. Cook almonds over low heat in sugar, stirring occasionally. Cool on wax paper. Place all ingredients together and toss. Use sweet-sour dressing.

Sweet-Sour Dressing

¼ cup vegetable oil
2 T. sugar
2 T. vinegar

1 T. snipped parsley
½ tsp. salt
dash pepper

Shake all ingredients in a tightly covered jar; refrigerate.

MEDITERRANEAN PASTA SALAD

Barbara Haberly

(8-oz.) bow tie pasta
1 cup cucumber slices, quartered
⅓ cup Kalamata or ripe olives, chopped

1 (7-oz.) jar roasted red pepper, drained and chopped
¾ cup crumbled Feta cheese
½ cup sliced green onion
Greek Dressing (recipe below)

Cook pasta according to package directions, drain. Cool (rinse with cold water to cool quickly). Prepare Greek dressing and pour over pasta, mixing well. Stir in remaining ingredients.

Greek Dressing

½ cup Italian Salad Dressing
3 T. fresh lemon juice

1 tsp. dried oregano leaves
¼ tsp. ground cinnamon

Stir all ingredients together.

64809B-05

MEXICAN SALAD

Jane Miller, Winship Volunteer

1 bag lettuce, chopped
(15-oz.) can red or kidney beans
2 tomatoes, diced
½ sm. onion, diced
1 lg. green pepper. diced

(10-oz.) pkg. grated cheddar
  cheese
(10-oz.) bag corn chips, crushed
(6-oz.) Kraft Catalina Salad
  Dressing

Makes 6 servings. Drain and rinse beans. In a large bowl, mix lettuce, beans, tomatoes, onions, peppers and cheese. Chill for 1 hour. Just before serving, toss with dressing and add corn chips.

MYSTERY SALAD

Mary Ellen Barbazon, Winship Volunteer

1 can stewed tomatoes
1 (3-oz.) pkg. lemon Jello
¾ cup water
½ cup diced green pepper

1 cup diced celery
1 med. onion, diced
¾ cup mayo

Makes 6 to 8 servings. Boil tomatoes and water. Add Jello (do not boil). Chill. Add the remaining ingredients. Good with vegetables or sandwich.

NO FAIL POTATO SALAD

Debbie Foster, Winship Volunteer

6 to 8 med. potatoes
3 to 4 boiled eggs
1 bunch green onions, chopped
1 cup mayonnaise (Hellmann's
  or Duke's)
1 T. sugar

1 T. apple cider vinegar
1 T. mustard
1 T. French dressing
seasoned salt, celery salt and
  onion salt to taste

Makes 6 to 8 servings. Cook potatoes and dice after skin is removed. Add diced eggs and green onions. Mix mayo, sugar, vinegar, mustard, and French dressing. Mix all together and season with celery salt and onion salt. (Season salt is optional, as is shredded carrots for color).

64809B-05

ORIENTAL CHICKEN SALAD

Jeanne Anderson, Winship Volunteer
Original source: Sandy Tatum

6 chicken breast halves
1-inch thick slices of fresh
  ginger
3 T. sugar
2 tsp. salt
½ tsp. pepper
¼ cup vinegar

½ cup vegetable oil
1 sm. head lettuce, shredded
4 cup fried won tons
4 green onions thinly sliced
(2-oz.) slivered almonds
¼ cup sesame seeds, toasted

Makes 8 servings. Cook chicken in water with ginger. Cool, bone and slice. Combine salt, sugar, pepper and vinegar in a small sauce pan. Cook over low heat until sugar is melted. Cool. Add oil and mix well. Toss all ingredients. Very light.

SAUERKRAUT SALAD

Debbie Foster, Winship Volunteer

2½ lb. pkg. sauerkraut,
  shredded (rinse and drain)
½ cup sugar
⅔ cup cider vinegar

1 cup chopped celery
1 cup chopped green pepper
1 cup chopped onion
1 sm. jar diced pimento

Makes 6 to 8 servings. Rinse sauerkraut. Boil sugar and vinegar until clear. Combine with remaining ingredients. Add celery salt to taste. Refrigerate for up to two weeks. Excellent with hot dogs as special side dish for cookouts.

SHRIMP SALAD

Eleanor Brownfield

1 lb. frozen white shrimp, 26 to
  30 count
about ⅛ cup thinly diced Vidalia
  onion
about ⅛ cup thinly sliced celery
about 1 tsp. sweet or dill pickle
  relish, drained

2 hard-cooked eggs, chopped
½ pinch powdered garlic
½ pinch dried dill seed
pinch coarse black pepper
about 1½ T. mayonnaise

Makes 4 to 6 servings. Cook shrimp according to package directions, without any spices--do not overcook. Drain and chill. Peel shrimp and cut each one into thirds or fourths. Dice vegetables; chop eggs. Gently combine all ingredients. Adjust seasonings and mayonnaise to taste.

64809B-05

TABBOULEH (LEBANESE BULGUR SALAD)

Stella Kazazian, Winship Volunteer

½ cup fine bulgur
¾ cup hot water
1 med. onion, finely chopped
½ cup finely chopped green onions (green and part parts)
1 cup finely chopped Italian parsley
½ cup finely chopped fresh mint

1½ cups chopped ripe tomatoes
⅓ cup strained fresh lemon juice
½ cup olive oil
½ tsp. salt
½ tsp. fresh ground black pepper

In a large bowl, soak the bulgur in hot water for at least 1 hour or until wheat is soft. May need to add more hot water or strain if water is standing in bowl. Wheat needs to be as dry as possible. Mix in the onion, green onions, tomatoes, parsley and mint. In a small bowl, combine the lemon juice, olive oil, salt and pepper; beat with a fork or whisk until well blended. Pour dressing into salad and mix. Taste for seasoning. Let salad stand for at least 1 hour before serving. Check again for seasoning. Serve on a bed of lettuce if desired.

NOTE: Bulgur or cracked wheat can be found in most markets, health food stores and farmers markets.

BREADS

"SWEETNESS BISCUITS"

Linda Appleton
Original Source:Walter "Sweetness" Payton's mother

2 cups low protein, self-rising flour

⅓ cup vegetable shortening
1 cup milk

Makes 18 servings. Preheat oven to 400°. Make well in flour and work shortening in by hand. Gradually add milk to mixture to make dough. Roll out dough on floured surface, being careful not to incorporate too much flour and not to work dough too much. Cut out biscuits and bake 8 to 10 minutes on greased baking sheet until well browned.

64809B-05

APPLE MUFFINS

Tiffany Barrett

²/₃ cup water
(7-oz.) apple cinnamon muffin
  mix
²/₃ cup oat bran

¾ cup cooked or canned pinto
  beans puréed or mashed
½ cup raisins
⅓ cup applesauce

Preheat oven to 400°. Pour water into mixing bowl and add muffin mix, oat bran and pinto beans; mix well. Fold in raisins and applesauce. Scoop into greased muffin pan. Sprinkle with cinnamon and sugar. Bake for 25 to 27 minutes for regular sized muffins.

BAKED FRENCH TOAST

Mary Metz
Original source: Sandy Metz

1 sm. loaf French bread (day
  old)
3 eggs
3 T. sugar
1 tsp. vanilla
2¼ cup milk

½ cup flour
6 T. dark brown sugar
½ tsp. cinnamon
¼ cup butter or margarine
1 cup blueberries & strawberries

Makes 8 servings. Cut bread in 1-inch slices and place in a greased 9 x 13 baking dish. Beat eggs, sugar and vanilla. Stir in milk and blend. Pour mixture over bread. Turn slices to coat well. Cover and refrigerate overnight. Combine flour, brown sugar, and cinnamon. Cut in butter or margarine until mixture resembles coarse crumbs. Turn bread slices over. Scatter blueberries over bread and sprinkle with crumb mixture. Set the oven to 375°. Bake 40 minutes. Cut into squares and top with strawberries.

All the answers to all the questions I shall ever ask are already within me.

64809B-05

BANANA BREAD

Julie Whitehead, Winship Volunteer
Interpreted from Doris Jarbeau

2 eggs
3 med. ripe bananas
²/₃ cup sugar
¹/₃ cup oil
¹/₂ cup chopped nuts

1³/₄ cups sifted all-purpose flour
2 tsp. baking powder
¹/₄ tsp. baking soda
¹/₂ tsp. salt

Makes 1 loaf. Break eggs into medium bowl; beat until well blended. Cut the bananas in 1-inch pieces, mash with eggs and mix well. Add sugar and oil to banana mixture and beat until well mixed. Sift flour, baking powder, baking soda, and salt together into banana mixture. Add nuts and milk until dry ingredients are just blended. Pour into greased 9¹/₂ x 5¹/₄ x 2³/₄ loaf pan. Bake at 350° for 55 to 60 minutes. Cool before cutting. Comes out perfect every time.

BANANA BREAD
(Diabetic Recipe)

Tiffany Barrett

1¹/₃ cups all-purpose flour
1 tsp. baking powder
¹/₂ tsp. baking soda
¹/₄ tsp. salt
¹/₂ cup Splenda Granular

1¹/₂ bananas, mashed
1 T. Canola oil
¹/₃ cup skim or 1% milk
2 tsp. vanilla
¹/₂ cup nuts, chopped

Preheat oven to 350°. Blend dry ingredients in a large bowl. Add oil, milk and vanilla to bananas; mix well. Pour banana mixture into dry ingredients. Stir until just mixed. Add chopped nuts. Pour batter into loaf pan coated with cooking spray. Bake for 45 minutes or until center is set.

64809B-05

BASIL BISCUITS

Linda Appleton

⅔ cup freshly grated Parmesan cheese, divided
2 cups all-purpose flour
2 tsp. baking powder
½ tsp. baking soda

8 T. unsalted butter, chilled, divided
⅓ cup finely chopped fresh basil (1 tablespoon dried)
¾ cup unflavored yogurt

Makes 7 servings. Preheat oven to 400°. Combine all but 2 tablespoons cheese with flour, baking powder, and baking soda. Add 7 tablespoons butter and rub with fingers until mixture resembles coarse crumbs. Stir in basil. Add yogurt and mix until dough clings together in lumps. Pat dough into ball and knead 10 times or until dough holds together. Gently form dough into 7-inch log and cut across into 7 equal pieces (for a rounded biscuit, roll each piece into a ball). Set 1 biscuit in center of buttered cake pan, then evenly space remaining biscuits around center. Melt remaining 1 tablespoon butter and brush over tops of biscuits. Sprinkle with reserved 2 tablespoons cheese. Bake until biscuits are golden brown--20 minutes. Serve hot.

BLUEBERRY BANANA LOAF

Helene Rabinowitch, Winship Volunteer

1 cup blueberries
1¾ cups all-purpose flour
2 tsp. baking powder
¼ tsp. baking soda
½ tsp. salt

⅓ cup margarine
⅔ cup sugar
2 eggs
1 cup mashed banana

Makes 1 loaf. Preheat oven to 350°. Toss the washed and drained blueberries with 2 tablespoons of the measured flour. Sift the remaining flour, baking powder, soda and salt together. Set aside. Cream the margarine and gradually beat in the sugar until fluffy. Beat in the eggs, one at a time. Add the flour mixture alternately with the banana, stirring until blended. Stir in the blueberries. Pour into greased and floured loaf pan. Bake for 50 to 60 minutes.

64809B-05

BLUEBERRY QUICK BREAD

Helene Rabinowitch, Winship Volunteer

5 cups all-purpose flour
2 T. baking powder
1 tsp. salt
1½ cups sugar
¾ cups margarine
4 eggs

2 cups milk
2 tsp. vanilla
3 cups blueberries
1½ cups chopped walnuts
  (optional)

Makes 2 loaves. Preheat oven to 350°. Sift flour, baking powder, salt and sugar together. Cut margarine into flour mixture as you would making pie dough. In a separate bowl thoroughly blend eggs, milk, and vanilla. Add blueberries and nuts if desired. (If you use frozen blueberries, it's better not to defrost them before adding to liquid ingredients). Grease two 9 x 5 loaf pans. Add wet ingredients to dry ingredients and blend together thoroughly but quickly. Pour batter into pans and put immediately into preheated oven. Bake for 75 minutes.

BRUSCHETTA

Stella Kazazian, Winship Volunteer

1 crusty Italian bread--slice on
  the diagonal ¼ inch to ½ inch
  thick
1 T. minced garlic
½ cup extra-virgin olive oil
3 cups fresh tomatoes, seeded
  and chopped
½ cup chopped fresh basil

salt and pepper to taste
2 T. red wine or balsamic
  vinegar
optional: mozzarella, red onion
  slices, fresh or dried oregano,
  Italian deli meats and
  Parmesan cheese, etc.

Brown both sides of the sliced bread under the broiler or on the grill. In a bowl, combine olive oil and garlic. Brush oil on one side of the bread. (Or brush oil on bread without the garlic, then broil and rub the toasted bread with a garlic clove cut in half). In a pan, heat remaining oil, add the tomatoes, vinegar to taste, salt and pepper. When all is just heated through, add basil and take off the heat. Put this mixture on the bread and serve. At this point, you can also put shredded mozzarella on top and return to broiler until cheese melts, or add any topping you want.

64809B-05

CAST-IRON SWEET CORNBREAD

George Rhone, Jr

2 cups corn meal
1⅓ cups milk
½ cup sugar

2 eggs (beaten)
2 T. margarine/butter
1 tsp. cooking oil

Makes 6 to 10 servings. Preheat oven to 450°. Coat the bottom and sides of your cast-iron skillet with 1 tablespoon of margarine or butter (do not melt). Beat your eggs in a cup. In a large mixing bowl, add cornmeal, beaten eggs, sugar, milk and oil. Mix well, with a large spoon or mixer, until batter is smooth and pours freely into your greased skillet. Place the skillet into your oven and leave it for 20 to 25 minutes, or until cornbread is golden brown and a toothpick inserted in the center comes out clean. Spread the remaining tablespoon of margarine or butter on the cornbread while it's still hot. Let it cool for 10 minutes before cutting into desired portions.

CHEESY BREAD

April Leach

1 loaf bakery French bread
1 (8-oz.) pkg. sliced Swiss
  cheese
2 T. onion, chopped

1 T. dry mustard
1 T. poppy seeds
1 tsp. seasoned salt
1 cup margarine, melted

Makes 8 servings. Using a serrated knife, cut diagonal slits in the bread, going almost all the way through. Put the bread on a large sheet of foil on a baking sheet. Place pieces of the Swiss cheese in the slits. Combine the last 5 ingredients and pour over the bread. Wrap the foil around the bread. Bake at 350° for 35 to 40 minutes. Serve warm.

I trust that wisdom will be given to me when I need it.

64809B-05

CINNAMON BREAD

Helene Rabinowitch, Winship Volunteer

2 cups all-purpose flour
1 cup sugar
¼ cup shortening
1 tsp. baking powder
1 tsp. baking soda

½ tsp. salt
1 tsp. vanilla
2 eggs
1 cup milk soured with 1
teaspoon vinegar

Topping

1 T. white sugar

1 T. cinnamon

Makes 1 loaf. Preheat oven to 375°. Cream shortening and sugar; mix in eggs, sour milk and vanilla. Add flour, soda, baking powder and salt. Grease loaf pan and add half of batter and sprinkle evenly with remaining topping. Bake in preheated oven for 35 to 40 minutes, then decrease the temperature to 350° and bake for 20 more minutes.

CORN MUFFINS

Helene Rabinowitch, Winship Volunteer

½ cup butter
1 cup sugar
2 eggs
1 cup yellow cornmeal

1½ cups all-purpose flour
2 tsp. baking powder
½ tsp. salt
1½ cups milk

Makes 12 muffins. In a mixing bowl, cream the butter and sugar together. Add the eggs; beat well, then add cornmeal. Sift the flour with baking powder and salt. Stir in alternately with the milk. Pour into a greased 8-inch square pan or into muffin tins. Bake at 375° for 15 to 17 minutes.

Variation: add 1¼ cups blueberries.

64809B-05

CRANBERRY BREAD

Helene Rabinowitch, Winship Volunteer

2½ cups all-purpose flour
1 cup milk
½ cup sugar
½ cup brown sugar, firmly
  packed
¼ cup oil
2 eggs

3 tsp. baking powder
½ tsp. baking soda
1 cup fresh or frozen
  cranberries
2 T. lemon juice or juice of one
  lemon

Makes 1 loaf. Preheat oven to 350°. Cream oil and sugar, add eggs. Mix in milk and lemon juice. In a separate bowl combine ingredients together until well moistened and pour into a greased loaf pan. Bake for 60 to 65 minutes. Store loaf at least 8 hours before slicing.

CREAM CHEESE BRAIDS

Cheryl Collier

½ cup sugar
1 stick butter
1 cup sour cream
1 tsp. salt

½ cup water
2 pkgs. active yeast
2 eggs
4 cube plain flour

Cream butter and sugar. Add sour cream, salt, eggs and flour. Add yeast to warm water with a pinch of sugar. When yeast is activated add to mix. Refrigerate.

Filling

(2-oz.) pkgs. cream cheese
¾ cup sugar
1 egg

2 tsp. vanilla
⅛ tsp. salt

Mix all together. Take dough from refrigerator and roll out onto a floured surface. Cut into 4 strips. Parcel filling into each strip, fold and pinch. Cook for 12 to 15 minutes at 375°.

Icing

2 cup powdered sugar
1 tsp. vanilla

2 tsp. milk

Mix and drizzle over cooled cakes.

64809B-05

IRISH SODA BREAD

Shannon Sullivan

5 cups sifted all-purpose
  unbleached flour
3/4 cup sugar
2 tsp. baking powder
1 1/2 tsp. salt
1 tsp. baking soda
1 stick butter

2 1/2 cups mixed light and dark
  raisins, soaked in water for 15
  to 20 minutes, drained
3 T. caraway seeds
2 1/2 cups buttermilk
1 lg. egg, slightly beaten

Preheat oven to 350°. Generously butter 2 (9 x 5) bread pans. Stir together the sifted flour, sugar, baking powder, salt, and baking soda. Cut in the butter and mix very thoroughly with your hands until it gets grainy. Stir in raisins and caraway seeds. Add the buttermilk and egg to the flour mixture. Stir until well moistened. Shape dough into 2 loaves and place in the pans. Bake for 1 hour. Test with a toothpick for doneness. Cool in the pans for 3 to 5 minutes. Transfer to a wire rack to cool.

JUDY'S CHEDDAR CHEESE BREAD

Helene Rabinowitch, Winship Volunteer

8 cups all-purpose flour
8 tsp. baking powder
4 T. sugar
2 tsp. salt
1 cup hard margarine

4 cups grated cheddar cheese
2 tsp. dill weed
4 eggs
3 cups milk

Makes 3 loaves. Preheat the oven to 350°. Sift into large mixing bowl the flour, baking powder, sugar and salt. Cut in margarine until the mixture resembles coarse crumbs. Stir in cheese and dill weed; mix well. Add the eggs to the milk, pour into dry ingredients and stir quickly. Pour into greased loaf pans. Bake for 40 minutes.

MARLA'S POPPY SEED CAKE BREAD

Marla Cook

4 eggs
1 cup sour cream
1/2 cup oil
1/2 cup orange juice

1/3 cup poppy seed
1 box French Vanilla pudding
1 box yellow cake mix with
  pudding

Combine all ingredients. Pour into a greased loaf or bundt pan. Bake at 350° for 50 to 60 minutes. Let cool for 10 minutes, then turn out of pan to finish cooling.

64809B-05

MOIST PUMPKIN BREAD

Elizabeth Evans

1 can pumpkin (about 2 cups)
3 cups sugar
1 cup water
1 cup vegetable oil

4 eggs
3½ cups self-rising flour
3 tsp. cinnamon

Combine first 5 ingredients and mix with electric mixer. Add dry ingredients and mix. Put in greased loaf pan and cook on 350° until done (depending on the size of the pan).

PARMESAN MONKEY BREAD

Lynn Gibson

2 tubes refrigerated biscuits
2 cloves garlic
1 tsp. dry mustard

1 cup grated Parmesan cheese
2 cup melted margarine

Makes 8 servings. Crush the garlic and add melted margarine and dry mustard. Cut the biscuits into quarter pieces. Coat 4 tablespoons margarine in bottom of 9 x 13 pan. Scatter the biscuit pieces over the pan. Top with remaining melted margarine mixture, and sprinkle with Parmesan cheese. Bake at 375° for 12 minutes, or until golden brown.

PEAR BREAD

Helene Rabinowitch, Winship Volunteer

½ cup soft margarine
1 cup sugar
2 eggs
2 cups all-purpose flour
½ tsp. salt
½ tsp. baking soda

1 tsp. baking powder
⅛ tsp. nutmeg
¼ cup buttermilk
1 cup coarsely chopped pears
1 tsp. vanilla

Makes 1 loaf. Preheat oven to 350°. In a mixing bowl, cream the butter. Gradually beat in the sugar. Beat in the eggs, one at a time. In a separate bowl combine the dry ingredients. Alternately add the dry ingredients and the buttermilk to the egg mixture. Stir in the pears and vanilla. Pour into greased loaf pan and bake for 40 minutes to 1 hour.

64809B-05

PINEAPPLE BANANA LOAF

Helene Rabinowitch, Winship Volunteer

3 cups all-purpose flour
2 cups sugar
1 tsp. baking powder
1 tsp. baking soda
1 tsp. salt
1 cup undrained crushed
 pineapple

3 eggs
1½ cups corn or canola oil
2 cups mashed banana (about 5
 bananas)
2 tsp. vanilla

Makes 2 loaves. Preheat oven to 350°. Mix in a large bowl the pineapple, eggs, oil, bananas and vanilla until blended. In a separate bowl combine flour, sugar, baking powder, baking soda and salt. Add dry ingredients to wet until thoroughly combined. Pour batter into greased loaf pans, dividing equally. Bake for 70 minutes. Cool for 15 minutes in pan then remove to rack.

PINEAPPLE ZUCCHINI LOAF

Helene Rabinowitch, Winship Volunteer

3 eggs
2 cups granulated sugar
1 cup corn or canola oil
3 T. vanilla
2 cups grated/puréed zucchini
1 cup crushed pineapple,
 undrained

3 cups flour
1 tsp. baking powder
1 tsp. baking soda
1 tsp. cinnamon
1 tsp. nutmeg
1 tsp. salt

Makes 2 loaves. Mix eggs, sugar, oil, vanilla, crushed pineapple and zucchini. In a separate bowl mix flour, baking powder, baking soda, cinnamon, nutmeg and salt. Combine wet and dry ingredients. Pour into bread pans and bake at 325° for 50 to 60 minutes. Remove from pan and let cool completely. Loaf is moist and dense.

I see my problems as opportunities.

64809B-05

PLUM BREAD

Helene Rabinowitch, Winship Volunteer

½ cup butter or margarine
1 cup sugar
½ tsp. vanilla
2 eggs
1½ cups all-purpose flour
½ tsp. salt
½ tsp. cream of tartar

¼ tsp. baking soda
⅓ cup plain yogurt
½ tsp. grated lemon peel
1 cup diced plums
½ cup chopped walnuts
(optional)

Makes 1 loaf. Preheat oven to 350°. Cream together the butter, sugar and vanilla until fluffy. Add the eggs one at a time; beat after each addition. Into a separate mixing bowl sift the flour, salt, cream of tartar and soda. Blend the yogurt and lemon peel. Alternately add yogurt mixture and dry mixture to the creamed mixture. Stir until well blended. Add plums and walnuts; mix well. Pour into greased loaf pan. Bake for 80 minutes.

PUMPKIN LOAF

Helene Rabinowitch, Winship Volunteer

3 cups sugar
3 cups brown sugar, firmly
 packed
2 cups oil
6 eggs
4 cups pumpkin purée
6 cups all-purpose flour

3 tsp. ground cloves
3 tsp. cinnamon
1 tsp. allspice
3 tsp. nutmeg
1 tsp. baking powder
2 tsp. baking soda
1 tsp. salt

Makes 3 loaves. Preheat oven 350°. Mix together sugars and oil. Beat in eggs and pumpkin. Sift together remaining ingredients in separate bowl then add to creamed mixture. Blend well. Pour into lightly greased pan. You may add raisins or chopped nuts if desired. Bake for 60 to 75 minutes.

64809B-05

RAISIN BRAN MUFFINS

Jane Miller, Winship Volunteer

(15-oz.) pkg. Raisin Bran cereal
1 cup Wesson or Crisco oil
2 cups sugar
5 tsp. baking soda
2 tsp. salt

4 eggs beaten
1 qt. buttermilk
5 cups flour
hand full of raisins

Makes 24 servings; 4 dozen muffins. Mix all together. Bake in muffin pans as needed. Bake at 400° for 25 minutes (or less). Baked muffins freeze well; batter will keep in the refrigerator for 2 to 3 weeks.

RAISIN LOAF

Helene Rabinowitch, Winship Volunteer

2 cups raisins
2 cups water
¾ cups shortening
2 cups sugar
1 egg
½ tsp. vanilla

4 cups all-purpose flour
1 tsp. nutmeg
½ tsp. cloves
¼ tsp. salt
2 tsp. baking soda
1 tsp. cinnamon

Makes 2 loaves. Preheat oven to 350°. Boil raisins in water for 5 minutes. Add 1 cup cold water and set aside to cool. In a mixing bowl cream together shortening, sugar, egg and vanilla. Add raisins and water. Sift together flour, nutmeg, cloves, salt, soda and cinnamon. Add gradually to the wet mixture, stirring until blended. Pour into greased and floured loaf pans. Bake for 1 hour.

I relax and know that all is well.

64809B-05

RHUBARB LOAF

Helene Rabinowitch, Winship Volunteer

2¼ cups all-purpose flour
1 cup whole-wheat flour
2 tsp. baking soda
1 tsp. baking powder
1 tsp. salt
2 tsp. cinnamon
½ tsp. nutmeg

½ tsp. allspice
3 eggs
1 cup vegetable oil
1½ cups brown sugar
2 tsp. vanilla extract
2½ cups diced rhubarb
½ cup chopped nuts (optional)

Makes 2 loaves. Preheat oven 350°. Beat the eggs, oil, brown sugar, and vanilla in a large bowl until light and fluffy. In a separate bowl combine flours, baking soda, baking powder, salt, and spices. Stir into wet mixture until just moistened. Stir in rhubarb and nuts. Pour into greased loaf pans and bake. Allow to cool 10 minutes before removing from pans.

ROSEMARY-FENNEL BREADSTICKS

Judy Baker
Interpreted from "Good Housekeeping: A Very Merry Christmas Cookbook 2003"

2 pkgs. quick rise yeast
2½ tsp. salt
2 tsp. fennel seeds, crushed
1 tsp. dried rosemary, crumbled
½ tsp. coarsely ground black pepper

about 4 to ¾ cups all-purpose flour
1⅓ cups very warm water (120° to 130°)
½ cup olive oil

Makes 64 breadsticks. In large bowl combine yeast, salt, fennel seeds, rosemary, pepper and 2 cups flour. With spoon, stir in warm water; beat vigorously with spoon 1 minute. Stir in oil. Gradually stir in 2¼ cups flour. Turn dough onto floured surface and knead until smooth and elastic--about 8 minutes, working in more flour (about ½ cup) while kneading. Cover dough loosely with plastic wrap; let rest 10 minutes. Preheat oven to 375°. Grease 2 large cookie sheets. Divide dough in half. Keeping one-half of dough covered, cut other half into 32 pieces. Shape each piece into 12-inch long rope. Place ropes, about 1-inch apart, on cookie sheets. Place cookie sheets on 2 oven racks and bake breadsticks 20 minutes, or until golden and crisp throughout, rotating cookie sheets between upper and lower racks halfway through baking time. Transfer breadsticks to wire racks to cool. Repeat with remaining dough.

64809B-05

ST. JOHN'S BANANA BREAD

Jane Miller, Winship Volunteer

½ cup butter or margarine
1 cup sugar
2 eggs
2 cups sifted flour
1 T. melted butter

1 tsp. baking soda
½ tsp. salt
3 lg. bananas, mashed
1 cup chopped nuts
Cinnamon/sugar mixture

Makes 1 loaf. Cream butter and sugar. Beat in eggs, one at a time. Mix in sifted flour, and dry ingredients. Beat in mashed bananas. Add nuts. Bake at 350° for 50 to 60 minutes. While bread is still warm, pour melted butter over top and sprinkle with cinnamon and sugar.

ZUCCHINI BREAD

Jane Miller, Winship Volunteer

3 cups flour
2½ cups sugar
1 T. baking soda
½ tsp. baking powder
1 tsp. salt
1 T. cinnamon

1 cup nuts
2 cups zucchini, peeled and
  grated
1 cup oil
3 eggs
1 T. vanilla

Makes 2 loaves. Beat eggs. Add oil and mix. Add zucchini and vanilla. Mix dry ingredients and add to mixture. Add nuts. Grease and flour two bread pans. Bake one hour at 350°.

Recipe Favorites

64809B-05

Recipe Favorites

64809B-05

Vegetables & Side Dishes

Helpful Hints

- When preparing a casserole, make an additional batch to freeze. It makes a great emergency meal when unexpected guests arrive. Just take the casserole from the freezer and bake it in the oven.

- To keep hot oil from splattering, sprinkle a little salt or flour in the pan before frying.

- Never overcook foods that are to be frozen. Foods will finish cooking when reheated. Don't refreeze cooked thawed foods.

- A few drops of lemon juice added to simmering rice will keep the grains separated.

- Green pepper may change the flavor of frozen casseroles. Clove, garlic, and pepper flavors get stronger when they are frozen, while sage, onion, and salt get milder.

- Don't freeze cooked egg whites; they become tough.

- For an easy no-mess side dish, grill vegetables along with your meat.

- When freezing foods, label each container with its contents and the date it was put into the freezer. Store at 0°. Always use frozen cooked foods within one to two months.

- Store dried pasta, rice (except brown rice), and whole grains in tightly covered containers in a cool, dry place. Always refrigerate brown rice, and refrigerate or freeze grains if they will not be used within five months.

- To dress up buttered, cooked vegetables, sprinkle them with toasted sesame seeds, toasted chopped nuts, canned french-fried onions, or slightly crushed seasoned croutons.

- Soufflé dishes are designed with straight sides to help your soufflé climb to magnificent heights. Ramekins are good for serving individual casseroles.

- A little vinegar or lemon juice added to potatoes before draining will make them extra white when mashed.

- To quickly bake potatoes, place them in boiling water for 10 to 15 minutes. Pierce their skins with a fork and bake in a preheated oven.

- To avoid toughened beans or corn, add salt midway through cooking.

VEGETABLES & SIDE DISHES

VEGETABLES

BAKED CORN

Susan Tomlin
Melanie Price

1 (15-oz.) can whole kernel corn, drained
1 (15-oz.) can cream style corn
1 cup sour cream

1 stick butter--no substitutes
2 eggs
1 box Jiffy corn bread mix

Makes 4 servings. Mix all ingredients well. Pour into a greased 9 x 13 baking dish. Bake 30 to 40 minutes at 350° or until edges are brown.

BAKED VIDALIA ONIONS

Betty Otto Matousek

4 lg. Vidalia onions, peeled and partially cooked
4 T. butter

seasoned salt
¾ cup Bloody Mary mix or tomato juice

Makes 4 servings. Place onions in oven proof dish with tight fitting lid. Place 1 tablespoon of butter in each onion core, sprinkle with seasoned salt to taste. Put a spoonful of juice on each onion and pour the rest around the onions. Cover and microwave for 10 minutes on high.

BASIL BUTTERED BEANS

Judy Baker
"Taste of Home's: Quick Cooking" November/December 2004

4 cups water
1 tsp. chicken bouillon granules
1½ lbs. fresh green beans, trimmed

1 to 2 T. butter, melted
¾ tsp. dried basil

Makes 4 servings. In a large saucepan, bring water and bouillon to a boil. Add the beans. Cook for 3 to 4 minutes or until crisp-tender; drain. Stir in butter and basil.

64809B-05

CABBAGE AND NOODLES (HUNGARIAN STYLE)

Elizabeth Anna Iski

1 med. head of shredded
  cabbage (approx. 4 cups)
1 lb. bacon cut into small pieces
1 cup finely sliced onion
1 T. salt

4 T. butter or vegetable oil
2 tsp. sugar
¼ tsp. pepper or to taste
3 cups cooked broad noodles

Mix the salt and cabbage in a large bowl and let stand for about 30 minutes. Squeeze out as much of the water as possible. Cook bacon until crisp in a large skillet and remove bacon. Drain off all bacon fat or leave 2 tablespoons for extra flavor. Add only 2 to 3 tablespoons of the butter or oil if using bacon fat and sauté onions until golden. Add cabbage, sugar, and pepper and cook over low heat, stirring frequently until cabbage is thoroughly cooked and even a bit browned. Add the noodles and stir until well mixed. Top with crispy bacon and serve. Great with pork and chicken.

CAULIFLOWER MOUNTAIN

Jean Seaverns

med. head cauliflower
½ cup mayonnaise
1½ tsp. prepared mustard

½ tsp. dry mustard
(2-oz.) sharp cheddar cheese,
  shredded

Makes 6 servings. Place whole head of cauliflower, stem side down, in an 8-inch glass pie plate. Cover completely with plastic wrap. Microwave on high for 8 minutes. Mix mayo and mustards and spread over cooked cauliflower. Sprinkle with shredded cheese. Microwave on high for 1 minute.

CORN PUDDING

Helene Rabinowitch, Winship Volunteer

1 lb. white or yellow corn,
  drained
3 tsp. flour
3 eggs, beaten
1½ cups evaporated milk

3 tsp. melted butter
4 tsp. sugar
dash of Tabasco, salt, and
  pepper

Mix ingredients. Pour into a 1½-quart greased baking dish. Bake at 325° for 1 hour. Sprinkle cheddar cheese on top (optional).

64809B-05

CREAMED SPINACH

Stella Kazazian, Winship Volunteer
Original Source: "The Best of Georgia Farms--
Cookbook and Tour Book"

4 bacon slices, finely chopped
1 cup chopped onion
1/4 cup all-purpose flour
2 tsp. seasoned salt
1/2 tsp. seasoned pepper

1/2 tsp. garlic powder
1 1/2 to 2 cups milk
2 (10-oz.) pkgs. chopped frozen
   spinach, cooked and drained
   well

Makes 8 servings. In a medium skillet, cook bacon until almost crisp; add onion. Cook until onion is tender; remove from heat. Add flour and seasonings; gradually add in milk, starting with 1 1/2 cups. Add spinach and mix thoroughly. If too thick, add remaining milk.

EGGPLANT PARMESAN

Helene Rabinowitch, Winship Volunteer

2 med. eggplants, peeled and
   cut in 1/2-inch slices (12 slices)
2 onions, sliced into rings
1 (28-oz.) can crushed tomatoes,
   undrained

1 tsp. dried oregano leaves
1/2 tsp. dried basil leaves
salt and pepper to taste
1 (8-oz.) pkg. part skim
   mozzarella cheese, shredded

Makes 4 to 5 servings. Preheat oven to 350°. Broil eggplant slices 5-inches from heat, about 5 minutes or until brown on one side. Arrange slices, brown side down, in a 2-quart long casserole dish coated with nonstick cooking spray. Top with onions. In a food processor, combine tomatoes with juice, oregano, basil, salt and pepper, chopping into small pieces. Pour over eggplant. Bake for 45 minutes. Top with mozzarella cheese and bake an additional 15 minutes.

I am strong in body, mind and spirit.

64809B-05

EGGPLANT, RED PEPPER, AND FETA GRATIN

Mary Booth Thomas, Winship Volunteer

3 red bell peppers
2 lbs. eggplant, peeled and cut into ½ inch slices
5 T. olive oil
2 med. onions sliced thin

3-4 garlic cloves, minced
½ cup loosely packed fresh basil leaves
½ cup crumbled feta cheese

Char bell peppers over an open flame or broil them in the oven about 2-inches from the heat. Turn them every 5 minutes until their skin is blackened. Transfer them to a bowl and let stand, covered, until cool enough to handle. Peel peppers and rinse off the burned particles. Discard seeds and ribs and cut into ½-inch slices, reserving liquid in the bowl. Half eggplant slices if they are large. Cook in a pot of boiling water until tender, about 5 to 10 minutes. Drain. Preheat oven to 350°. Heat 2 tablespoons of oil in a skillet and cook onions and garlic, stirring occasionally. Spread onion mixture in the bottom of a shallow baking dish. Arrange a row of eggplant slices over the onion mixture and slip a basil leaf between each slice. Top with a row of pepper slices and continue alternating rows until you use up all the eggplant, basil and peppers. (Season vegetables with salt and pepper as you go). Drizzle reserved pepper water and 3 tablespoons of olive oil over veggies. Bake in the middle of the oven for 45 minutes. Sprinkle feta over vegetables and bake until the cheese is melted.

FIVE-VEGETABLE MEDLEY

Judy Baker
"Taste of Home's: Quick Cooking" November/December 2004

2 med. parsnips, peeled and julienned
2 med. carrots, julienned
2 celery ribs, julienned
1 sm. turnip, peeled and julienned

2 T. butter
1 med. sweet red pepper, julienned
½ cup white wine or chicken broth

Makes 6 servings. In a large skillet, sauté the parsnips, carrots, celery and turnip in butter for 5 minutes. Add red pepper; cook and stir 1 minute longer. Add wine or broth. Bring to a boil. Reduce heat; cover and simmer for 4 to 6 minutes or until vegetables are tender. Serve with a slotted spoon.

64809B-05

FREEZER FRESH CREAMED CORN

Barbara Faro

3 (16-oz.) pkgs. frozen corn
(white shoepeg), partially
thawed and divided
½ cup butter

1¾ to 2 cups milk
1½ to 2 tsp. salt
½ tsp. pepper

Makes 6 servings. Process 1 package of corn until smooth in food processor. Melt butter in a large heavy skillet--medium heat. Stir in all corn and remaining ingredients. Reduce heat and simmer 20 to 25 minutes until thickened and heated through.

GLAZED CARROTS

Julie Whitehead, Winship Volunteer
Original source: Jamie Grant

3 cups sliced carrots, cooked
and drained
2 T. butter
¼ cup brown sugar

2 T. prepared mustard
¼ tsp. salt
1 T. parsley

Makes 4 servings. Melt butter in skillet; stir in brown sugar, mustard, and salt. Add cooked carrots; beat, stirring constantly until carrots are nicely glazed (about 5 minutes). Sprinkle with parsley.

64809B-05

GREEN BEANS WITH HONEY-PECAN BUTTER

Judy Baker
Interpreted from "Good Housekeeping: A Very Merry
Christmas Cookbook 2003"

½ cup pecans
½ cup butter or margarine,
  softened
2 T. honey

½ tsp. coarsely ground black
  pepper
2 lbs. green beans, trimmed

Makes 8 servings. Preheat oven to 375°. Bake nuts in 8 x 8 metal baking pan; bake 8 to 10 minutes, until lightly toasted. Cool completely. In a food processor, with knife blade attached, process pecans until finely ground. In a bowl, mix butter with honey, pepper, and ground pecans until blended. Spoon mixture into a 6-inch long strip on a sheet of plastic wrap or waxed paper. Freeze about 20 minutes, until slightly firm. Roll mixture, covered with plastic wrap or waxed paper, back and forth to make a 6-inch long log. Wrap well; refrigerate up to 2 days or freeze up to 2 months (thaw in refrigerator 1 hour before using). In 12-inch skillet, heat ½-inch water and green beans to boiling over high heat. Reduce heat; simmer 5 to 10 minutes, until beans are just tender-crisp. Drain; rinse with cold running water to stop cooking. Transfer beans to zip-tight plastic bag and refrigerate up to 2 days if not serving right away. To serve: in 12-inch skillet, heat cooked beans with ¼ of pecan butter over medium heat until butter melts and beans are hot.

IMPOSSIBLE GARDEN PIE

Mary Kay Howard

2 cups chopped zucchini
1 cup chopped tomato
½ cup chopped onion
½ cup grated Parmesan cheese
1½ cups milk

¾ cup Bisquick
3 eggs
½ tsp. salt
¼ tsp. pepper

Preheat oven to 400°. Grease a 10-inch pie pan. Sprinkle zucchini, tomato, onion and cheese in pan. Beat remaining ingredients until smooth (about 15 seconds in a blender); pour in pan. Bake for 30 minutes. Let stand 5 minutes.

64809B-05

■■■■■■■■■■■■■■■

LEMONY BRUSSELS SPROUTS

Judy Baker
"Taste of Home's: Quick Cooking" November/December
2004

1 lb. fresh Brussels sprouts,
  trimmed and halved
2 T. water
2 T. butter, melted
2 T. lemon juice

2 tsp. grated lemon peel
¼ tsp. salt
¼ tsp. lemon-pepper seasoning
¼ cup sliced almonds, toasted

Makes 4 servings. Place the Brussels sprouts in a microwave-safe dish; add water. Cover and cook on high for 7 to 9 minutes or until tender, stirring twice; drain. Stir in the butter, lemon juice, lemon peel, salt and lemon-pepper. Sprinkle with almonds.

MARINATED VEGETABLES

Tiffany Barrett

½ lb. asparagus
½ cup sliced mushrooms
1 cup sliced red bell pepper
  strips
1 can artichoke hearts
1 cup carrots
2 cups small red potatoes,
  halved

¼ cup white wine vinegar
2 T. chopped fresh parsley
1 T. olive oil
1 tsp. dried oregano
½ tsp. sugar
¼ tsp. salt
½ tsp. pepper
1 garlic clove, minced

Steam potatoes, covered for 6 minutes or until tender. Steam asparagus, mushrooms, bell pepper and carrots for 3 to 6 minutes or until tender. Add drained artichoke hearts. Combine vinegar and remaining ingredients in a small bowl; stir well. Pour vinaigrette over the vegetables. Cover and marinate for 2 hours. Other vegetables may be substituted.

I relax and know that all is well.

■■■■■■■■

64809B-05

ONION PUDDING

Jean Seaverns

1 stick margarine
2 cups chopped onion
½ cup flour

1 cup evaporated milk
2 eggs, beaten
salt and pepper to taste

Makes 6 servings. Sauté onion in margarine until golden. Add flour and seasonings; blend in. Add milk gradually, stirring constantly. Remove from heat and add beaten eggs. Pour into greased casserole dish. Bake at 425° for 30 to 45 minutes, until puffed up in center. Delicious with roast beef!

RITZ SQUASH CASSEROLE

Debbie Foster, Winship Volunteer
Original source: Mary Wilson

2 lbs. yellow squash
1 cup water
1 sm. onion, minced
2 T. butter

1½ cup shredded sharp cheese
1¼ cup crushed Ritz Crackers
4 pieces bacon cooked
2 eggs

Makes 6 to 8 servings. Slice and cook squash in water for only 15 minutes. Drain and mash. Drain again. Sauté onion and then combine with all other ingredients. Put in a 1½-quart casserole dish after spraying with cooking spray. Cook at 350° for an hour.

ROASTED ASPARAGUS

Mary Booth Thomas, Winship Volunteer

1 bunch small asparagus, tough
  stalks removed
2 T. olive oil

4 T. Pecorino or Parmesan
  cheese

Blanch asparagus in boiling water for 2 to 3 minutes. Drain. Place in baking dish and mix in olive oil. Sprinkle cheese on top. Heat in 350° oven until cheese is melted.

64809B-05

ROASTED CARROTS WITH BALSAMIC VINEGAR

Mary Booth Thomas, Winship Volunteer

1 (8-oz.) pkg. peeled baby
  carrots
3 T. olive oil

salt and pepper to taste
1/4 cup Balsamic vinegar

Put carrots in a shallow baking pan and coat with olive oil. Season. Bake in 350° oven until tender (about 45 minutes). Stir in Balsamic vinegar and cook 10 more minutes.

ROASTED VEGETABLES

Mary Booth Thomas, Winship Volunteer

1 fennel bulb (greens removed)
2 red bell peppers
1 lb. creamer or fingerling
  potatoes

olive oil
chopped fresh rosemary
salt and pepper

Cut fennel and peppers into small strips. Halve potatoes. Mix with olive oil and rosemary in baking dish. Add salt and pepper to taste. Bake at 400° about 40 minutes until vegetables are soft.

SAVORY MUSHROOM CUSTARD

Stella Kazazian, Winship Volunteer

1 cup chicken stock
1/2 cup cream
4 eggs
3/4 tsp. salt
1/2 tsp. paprika

1/8 tsp. grated nutmeg
1 T. parsley, chopped
2 T. butter
2 cups fresh mushrooms,
  chopped

Makes 8 servings. Preheat oven to 350°. Put stock, cream, eggs and seasonings into a large bowl and beat with a wire whisk. Melt butter and sauté mushrooms for 5 minutes; drain. Add mushrooms to egg mixture and pour into 8 small buttered custard cups or 1 large mold; place in a pan of hot water. Bake in the oven for 20 or 30 minutes, or until firm (a sharp knife inserted in the middle should come out clean).

64809B-05

SCALLOPED CORN

Jane Miller, Winship Volunteer

1½ cups corn
1 cup milk
2 T. butter
2 T. flour

1 tsp. salt
pepper
2 eggs, beaten
2 cups buttered crumbs

Makes 5 servings. Drain liquid from corn into a measuring cup and add enough milk to make 1 cup. Heat butter. Add flour, salt and pepper. Stir until blended. Slowly add liquid. Cook, stirring constantly until thickened. Remove from heat and add corn. Slowly add eggs, stirring constantly. Top with buttered crumbs and paprika. Place in shallow pan of water. Bake at 350° for 45 to 50 minutes.

SHOE PEG CORN

Nikki Elliott

3 (10-oz.) cans shoepeg corn
2 (15-oz.) cans French-cut green
  beans
1 (8-oz.) container sour cream

1 can cream of celery soup
½ cup chopped onion
salt and pepper to taste

Combine and mix ingredients in a 3-quart casserole dish. Cook at 350° for 30 minutes or until bubbly. Add topping and shredded cheese (to taste). Cook until cheese is melted.

Topping

1 sleeve Ritz crackers

1 stick butter or margarine

Crush crackers. Melt butter over medium heat. Add crackers and mix well.

I am filled with energy that attracts abundance into my life.

64809B-05

SPINACH CASSEROLE

Debbie Foster, Winship Volunteer

½ cup finely chopped onion
6 T. butter
¼ lb. sliced mushrooms or a
  small bottle sliced mushrooms
2 T. flour
½ cup water
(8-oz.) Velveeta Italian or pepper
  jack cheese

2 pkgs. frozen chopped spinach,
  thawed and drained
3 eggs beaten
6 slices cooked and crumbled
  bacon or 6 T. bacon pieces
½ cup soda cracker crumbs,
  crushed

Makes 4 to 6 servings. Sauté onion and mushrooms in 4 tablespoons of butter. Add flour and water to make paste. Then add cheese, chopped and drained spinach, and bacon pieces. Remove from heat to add eggs--blend and pour into a 1½-quart casserole dish. Cover with cracker crumbs and dot with remaining 2 tablespoons of butter. Bake at 350° for 45 to 55 minutes.

SPINACH ZUCCHINI POTATO PANCAKES

Nin Sciretta, Winship Volunteer

1 (10-oz.) frozen chopped
  spinach, thawed and squeezed
  dry
2 cups shredded zucchini
1 med. potato peeled and
  shredded

¼ cup finely chopped onion
¼ cup all-purpose flour
½ tsp. salt, pepper, and nutmeg
1 egg, beaten

Mix all ingredients together. Drop by ¼ cup in oil and fry until golden brown on both sides.

SQUASH CASSEROLE

Elaine Koenig

1 cup sour cream
1 sm. grated onion
salt and pepper to taste
1 pkg. seasoned bread crumbs
  (Pepperidge Farm)

2 cups cooked mashed squash
1 carrot, grated
2 eggs

Makes 6 servings. Mix all the ingredients except the bread crumbs. Sprinkle bread crumbs on the bottom of buttered casserole dish. Add squash mixture. Cover with more bread crumbs and add generous dots of butter. Bake at 350° for 30 minutes.

64809B-05

TEXAS SCALLOPED CORN

Sandra Murdock

1 tsp. red hot pepper sauce
1 stick oleo, melted
2 eggs
1 cup sour cream
1 box Jiffy cornbread mix

½ chopped onion
½ chopped green pepper
1 can cream style corn
1 can whole kernel corn, not
  drained

Makes 10 to 12 servings. Stir together the first 5 ingredients. Add the rest one at a time, stirring between. Put in a greased 9 x 13 pan and bake at 350° for 1 hour.

TOMATO PIE

Debbie Foster, Winship Volunteer

3 to 4 lg. tomatoes sliced or
  drain a can of tomatoes and
  slice
3 stalks celery, chopped
1 med. onion, chopped
6 slices crumbled bacon or 6 T.
  canned bacon pieces

1 cup mayonnaise
½ cup or more Parmesan
  cheese (do not use fresh or
  shredded)
salt and pepper taste
double pie crust

Makes 8 to 10 servings. Mix the first 6 ingredients. If the tomatoes are still soupy, add more Parmesan cheese. Pour into prepared pie crust and put top crust on ingredients. Make a few air holes. Cook in the oven at 350°, similar to baking an apple pie. May be served hot or cold.

64809B-05

ZUCCHINI WITH CITRUS-HERB DRESSING

Nin Sciretta, Winship Volunteer

1½ lbs. medium zucchini
½ tsp. salt
1 garlic clove, minced

2 T. olive oil
Garnish: lemon slices

Cut zucchini in half lengthwise, and cut into ¼-inch wedges about 1½-inches long. Sprinkle wedges evenly with salt. Sauté minced garlic in hot oil in a skillet over medium-high heat, until lightly browned. Add zucchini and cook, stirring occasionally, 8 to 10 minutes or until tender. Pour Citrus-Herb Dressing over zucchini, tossing to coat. Garnish, if desired. Serve immediately.

Citrus-Herb Dressing

3 T. chopped fresh basil
1 T. chopped fresh thyme
2 T. fresh orange juice
2 T. fresh lemon juice

1 tsp. Dijon mustard
¼ tsp. salt
¼ tsp. pepper

Whisk all ingredients together in a medium bowl.

SIDE DISHES

"THE BEST BAKED BEANS"

Claire Smith
Original source: A very dear friend in North
Carolina

4 sm. cans Libby Baked Beans
5 T. Worcestershire sauce
5 T. brown sugar

1 cup catsup
1 lb. ground sirloin
3 lg. onions chopped

Makes 8 servings. Brown sirloin and onion. Pour off fat and add baked beans, Worcestershire sauce, brown sugar and catsup. Bake for 1 hour at 325° to 350°, or cook on low on top of stove.

64809B-05

BAKED ALL THE BEANS

Anne Evans

1 can green beans, drained
1 can wax beans, drained
1 can lima beans, drained
1 can kidney beans, drained
1 can pork 'n' beans, undrained
1 can chili beans, undrained

1 lb. sausage, brown and drain
½ to ¾ bottle of your favorite
  barbeque sauce
2 T. chili powder
¼ cup brown sugar

Makes 6 to 8 servings. Mix all ingredients together. Bake at 350° for 45 minutes or until bubbly.

BAKED MACARONI AND CHEESE (WITH OR WITHOUT HAM)

Mary Leigh Harper

2 T. cornstarch
1 tsp. salt
½ tsp. dry mustard (optional)
¼ tsp. pepper
2½ cups milk
2 T. margarine or butter

2 (8-oz.) cups shredded
  American or Cheddar cheese,
  diced
(8-oz.) elbow macaroni (about
  1¾ cups) cooked 7 minutes
  and drained

Makes 4 to 6 servings. In medium saucepan, combine the first 4 ingredients; stir in milk. Add butter, stirring constantly, bring to a boil over medium-high heat and boil 1 minute. Remove from heat. Stir in 1¾ cup cheese until melted. Add macaroni. Pour into greased 2-quart casserole dish. Sprinkle with reserved cheese. Bake at 375° uncovered in oven for 25 minutes or until lightly browned. For baked ham n' cheese macaroni, stir in 2 cups diced ham with macaroni.

All things work together for the greater good of all.

64809B-05

BEANS, PASTA, AND GREENS

Norman Heckert

2 cans non-fat great northern
beans
1 (6-oz.) can tomato paste
4 pkts. goya jamon seasoning
(ham) available in most
markets in the Mexican or
ethnic food section
extra virgin olive oil

crushed red pepper flakes
1 sm. onion
1 lg. carrot
1 stalk celery
3 cloves garlic
1 bunch kale
Parmesan cheese
any small tubular pasta (ditalini)

In a 3 or 4-quart sauce pot, heat 1 tablespoon olive oil over moderate heat. Finely chop or dice onion, carrot and celery; add to pot, sautéing until vegetables are cooked (approximately 8 to 10 minutes). Add minced garlic and cook until it gives off its essence. Add ½ teaspoon crushed red pepper flakes and ⅓ can of the tomato paste (open both ends of the can and push out plastic wrap, taking your ⅓ and rolling the remainder up and freezing it). Cook this mixture making sure that the paste is incorporated into the vegetables and slightly browned. Open beans and place 1½ cans along with any liquid into the pot. Add 2 cans of water to the pot; with a fork, mash the remaining beans and add to the pot. Allow to come to a simmer and add the ham seasonings, stirring to mix. Coarsely chop the kale until you have 4 or 5 handfuls. Add the chopped kale and stir and cook for 5 minutes. Now add 1 cup of pasta and cook until tender (10 to 15 minutes). Make sure to keep stirring frequently to keep pasta from sticking. Serve with a drizzle of the olive oil and a generous amount of grated Parmesan cheese. If the soup is too thick you may thin it a little with hot water.

DEVILED EGGS

Karin Brown

6 hard-boiled eggs
½ tsp. salt

½ tsp. dry mustard
3 T. mayonnaise

Cut peeled eggs lengthwise into halves. Slip out yolks; mix all ingredients. Fill whites with egg mixture.

64809B-05

EASY MACARONI AND CHEESE

Lynn Gibson

2 cups macaroni, uncooked
4 T. flour
1½ tsp. salt
2 cups water

2 cups milk
4 T. margarine
2 dashes Tabasco sauce
2 cups grated yellow cheese

Makes 4 servings. Preheat oven to 350°. Grease a medium baking dish and combine all ingredients except cheese in the dish and stir until well mixed. Bake covered for 30 minutes, or until macaroni is tender--stirring occasionally. Stir in cheese and bake uncovered for 5 minutes.

FRIED RICE

Caryn Shulman

1 cup cooked white rice
½ onion, chopped
2 cloves garlic, crushed
1 sm. box frozen mixed veggies
  (cooked)

½ cup sliced mushrooms
4 T. soy sauce
salt and pepper to taste

Makes 6 servings. In large frying pan, sauté garlic, onions, and mushrooms in 2 tablespoons of margarine or butter. Add rice and mixed veggies. Allow to slightly brown on one side; stir rice frequently. Add soy sauce and serve.

GARLIC GRITS

Elaine Scales

1 cup grits
5 cups water
1 tsp. salt
1 stick butter

2 to 3 cloves garlic finely
  chopped
1 lb. cheddar cheese grated
cayenne pepper to taste

Makes 6 to 8 servings. Bring the grits to a boil and then simmer until done, approximately 15 minutes. Add the remaining ingredients. Mix together and bake at 350° in a greased baking dish for 1 hour.

64809B-05

PARTYTIME BAKED BEANS

Mary and Becky Wilson

1½ cups ketchup
1 med. onion, chopped
1 med. green pepper, chopped
1 med. red pepper, chopped
½ cup water
½ cup brown sugar
2 bay leaves
2 to 3 T. cider vinegar
1 tsp. ground mustard
⅛ tsp. pepper

1 (16-oz.) can kidney beans,
  drained and rinsed
1 (15½-oz.) can great northern
  beans, drained and rinsed
1 (15-oz.) can lima beans,
  drained and rinsed
1 (15-oz.) can black beans,
  drained and rinsed
1 (15-oz.) can black eyed peas,
  drained and rinsed

Makes 8 servings. In slow cooker, combine the first 10 ingredients and mix well. Add beans and peas; mix well. Cook on low heat 5 to 7 hours. Remove bay leaves before serving.

PEG'S SWEET POTATO CASSEROLE

Debbie Hagood

1 lg. can sweet potatoes,
  drained
1 cup sugar
2 eggs

1 tsp. vanilla
½ cup butter softened
⅓ can evaporated milk (½ cup)

Mix above ingredients. Pour into a greased casserole dish with a cover. Bake 35 to 45 minutes at 350°.

Topping

¼ cup brown sugar
1 cup pecans

⅓ cup self rising flour
⅓ cup butter

Mix ingredients together. Spread topping evenly over casserole; bake another 10 minutes.

64809B-05

PINEAPPLE CASSEROLE I

Annette Beck

3 T. flour
½ cup sugar
1 cup sharp cheese, grated

1 (12-oz.) can crushed
  pineapples
3 T. pineapple juice

Mix flour, sugar, and pineapple juice. Fold in cheese and pineapple. Mix well. Pour into buttered casserole dish.

Topping

1 cup crushed Ritz crackers
  mixed with ½ stick melted
  margarine

Sprinkle topping over casserole. Bake 20 to 30 minutes at 350° until brown.

PINEAPPLE CASSEROLE II

Debbie Hagood

1 lg. can crushed pineapple,
  partially drained
¼ cup melted butter or
  margarine

¾ cup sugar
3 T. self rising flour
1 cup cheddar cheese, grated
Ritz crackers, crushed

Mix together pineapple, butter, sugar and flour. Add grated cheese and cover with Ritz crackers. Bake at 350° for 30 minutes.

POTATO CASSEROLE

Debbie Hagood

1½ lbs. frozen hash browns
½ cup chopped onion
½ lb. sharp cheddar cheese,
  grated
(16-oz.) sour cream
1 can cream of chicken soup

1 stick melted margarine
1 T. salt
dash of Tabasco
½ stick melted margarine
2 cups crushed corn flakes

Mix all ingredients together, except the last two ingredients. Pour into a casserole dish. Top with ½ stick melted margarine and 2 cups crushed corn flakes. Bake 1 hour at 350°.

Topping

½ stick melted margarine

2 cups crushed corn flakes

64809B-05

RATATOUILLE

Tallulah Kenyon
Original source: "What's Cooking at UUCA-Paula Walker"

1 lg. eggplant, diced (leave peel on or off)
2 green peppers, sliced in strips
1 lg. zucchini, diced (leave peel on or off)
1½ cup onions, thinly sliced
2 garlic buds, mashed
1 lb. tomatoes, sliced in strips
4 T. olive oil
3 T. minced parsley
1 tsp. salt
pepper and more oil if needed

Makes 8 servings. In some oil, sauté eggplant; set aside. Sauté peppers; set aside. Sauté zucchini; set aside. Sauté onions with garlic; set aside. Mix all ingredients in small Dutch oven. Cover and simmer over low heat for 10 minutes. Uncover and cook for 10 to 15 minutes. Chill for a salad or serve warm.

RICE WITH PEAS

Stella Kazazian, Winship Volunteer

½ cup oil or butter
½ cup sliced green onion, including green part
¼ cup minced parsley
1 (10-oz.) pkg. frozen peas
boiling salted water
4 cups cooked rice (brown rice can be used)
about 1⅓ cups of uncooked rice
2 tsp. grated lemon peel
2 T. soy sauce
hot pepper sauce to taste
salt and pepper to taste

Makes 4 to 6 servings. In a frying pan, heat oil or butter, add green onions and parsley; sauté until limp and bright green--about 2 to 3 minutes. Meanwhile, add peas to boiling water, bring back to a boil. Remove from heat, drain and set aside. Add rice, lemon zest, soy sauce, pepper sauce, peas, salt and pepper to frying pan. Stir carefully, until heated through.

I am filled with compassion for every living thing.

64809B-05

ROSEMARY POTATOES

Mary Booth Thomas, Winship Volunteer

1 lb. small potatoes (fingerlings, creamers, new potatoes or purple potatoes or a mixture)
2 lg. shallots, chopped

4 springs fresh rosemary, chopped fine
2 T. olive oil
salt and pepper

Cut potatoes in half and cook in boiling water until nearly done. Drain. Put in a casserole dish with shallots and coat with the olive oil. Add chopped rosemary and season with salt and pepper to taste. Cook at 400° until potatoes start to brown.

SWEET POTATO CASSEROLE

Joan and Joanna Seger

4 lbs. sweet potatoes
1 cup sugar
¼ cup milk
½ cup butter
2 eggs
1 tsp. vanilla extract

¼ tsp. salt
1¼ cups cornflakes, crushed
¼ cup pecans, chopped
1 T. brown sugar
1 T. butter, melted
1½ cups marshmallows

Makes 6 servings. Bake potatoes at 400° for 1 hour. Let cool; peel and mash. Beat mashed sweet potatoes, sugar and next 5 ingredients with electric mixer until smooth. Spoon into greased baking dish. Combine cornflakes and next 3 ingredients in a small bowl. Sprinkle diagonally over casserole in rows. Bake at 350° for 30 minutes. Let stand 10 minutes. Sprinkle alternate rows with marshmallows. Bake 10 additional minutes.

64809B-05

Entreés
& Casseroles

Helpful Hints

- Use little oil when preparing sauces and marinades for red meats. Fat from the meat will render out during cooking and will provide plenty of flavor. Certain meats, like ribs and pot roast, can be parboiled before grilling to reduce the fat content.

- When trying to reduce your fat intake, buy the leanest cuts you can find. Fat will show up as an opaque white coating or can also run through the meat fibers, as marbling. Although most of the fat (the white coating) can be trimmed away, there isn't much that can be done about the marbling. Stay away from well-marbled cuts of meat.

- Home from work late with no time for marinating meat? Pound meat lightly with a mallet or rolling pin, pierce with a fork, sprinkle lightly with meat tenderizer, and add marinade. Refrigerate for about 20 minutes, and you'll have succulent, tender meat.

- Marinating is a cinch if you use a plastic bag. The meat stays in the marinade and it's easy to turn and rearrange. Cleanup is easy; just toss the bag.

- It's easier to thinly slice meat if it's partially frozen.

- Tomatoes added to roasts will help to naturally tenderize them. Tomatoes contain an acid that works well to break down meats.

- Whenever possible, cut meats across the grain; they will be easier to eat and have a better appearance.

- When frying meat, sprinkle paprika over it to turn it golden brown.

- Thaw all meats in the refrigerator for maximum safety.

- Refrigerate poultry promptly after purchasing. Keep it in the coldest section of your refrigerator for up to two days. Freeze poultry for longer storage. Never leave poultry at room temperature for more than two hours.

- If you're microwaving skinned chicken, cover the baking dish with vented clear plastic wrap to keep the chicken moist.

- Lemon juice rubbed on fish before cooking will enhance the flavor and help maintain a good color.

- Scaling a fish is easier if vinegar is rubbed on the scales first.

ENTREES AND CASSEROLES

ENTREES

ARMENIAN MEAT PIZZA

Seda "Mom" Kazazian

Dough

2¼ cups sifted flour
¾ cup lukewarm water
1 env. rapid or fast action yeast

¼ cup vegetable oil
1 tsp. salt
½ tsp. sugar

Mix yeast with warm water and sugar; let stand until "bloomed". Add flour and salt to yeast mixture. Mix until you have a soft dough--add more flour if needed; add a little at a time until dough can be handled. Lightly oil hands and knead thoroughly for at least 10 minutes. Place dough in a oiled bowl, cover with towel and let stand in a warm place for at least 1 to 2 hours until doubled in size. *To make life easier, you can use store-bought dough. Make meat mixture while waiting.

Meat mixture

1 lb. ground lamb or ½ lamb
  and ½ ground sirloin
2 cups finely chopped onion
¼ cup finely chopped Italian
  parsley
½ sm. green pepper, finely
  chopped

salt and pepper to taste
1 tsp. fresh mint leaves
½ clove garlic (optional)
½ sm. can tomato paste
½ sm. can of whole tomatoes,
  drained and chopped

Preheat oven to 400°. Mix all the ingredients thoroughly by hand, until it resembles a paste. After the dough has risen, divide it into 12 egg size pieces and roll into a ball. Cover with a towel and let rest for 10 minutes. Roll or flatten each ball by hand, until 6 to 8-inch rounds on floured surface. Spread meat mixture thinly over the entire surface of each round. Place the "pizzas" on a greased pan (grease pan only once). Bake in a 400° oven for about 15 minutes or until meat is cooked and dough is lightly browned. These freeze beautifully.

64809B-05

BAKED CHICKEN BREASTS AND RICE

Sandra Murdock

¾ cup rice
1 pkg. dry onion soup mix
2 cans cream of chicken soup
8 chicken breasts, or legs and
  thighs

1 cup liquid (chicken broth, milk
  or wine)

Makes 6 to 8 servings. Mix all ingredients together, except chicken. Spread mixture in flat baking dish which has been lightly buttered. Place chicken on top. Dot with butter and sprinkle with paprika if desired. Bake 2 hours in 300° oven, covering with foil during the last hour.

BAKED SWISS CHICKEN

Linda Zimmerman, Winship Volunteer

1 whole chicken (can use pieces
  if you desire)
Dijon mustard
paprika

curry powder
poultry spice
seasoned salt

Rub whole chicken generously with Dijon mustard, coat well. Then sprinkle with paprika, curry powder, poultry spice and seasoned salt. Bake in 350° oven for 1½ hours. If desired, baste with butter for last half hour. Easy and delicious.

I live with passion.

64809B-05

BASQUE CHICKEN

Debbie Merk

6 lbs. chicken parts (breasts or breast and thighs)
½ cup flour and ½ cup bread crumbs
3 tsp. salt
½ tsp. pepper
¼ cup olive oil
2 garlic cloves minced or equivalent of minced garlic from jar
2 med. onions each cut into 8 wedges
1 med. red pepper slivered
1 med. green pepper slivered
1 lb. zucchini cut into 1-inch chunks
1½ tsp. oregano
½ tsp. basil
½ tsp. red pepper flakes
1 (16-oz.) can tomato chunks
1 cup white wine
1 (3¼-oz.) can pitted black olives drained and halved

Makes 8 servings. Mix flour, bread crumbs, salt and pepper; shake chicken in flour mixture; brown in olive oil by oven cooking at 400° until both sides are crispy. Remove chicken from pan and add enough oil to make ½ cup. Add garlic, onion wedges, red and green pepper. Cook in oven until tender-crisp (about 3 minutes); add 2 tablespoons of flour mixture and remaining spices (oregano, etc.), tossing to coat vegetables. Add canned tomatoes with liquid and wine; heat until bubbly in oven. Return chicken and zucchini. Bake at 350° for 30 minutes until chicken is tender. Uncover; add olives and serve. Goes well with either rice or pasta. To freeze remaining portion: spoon into a foil baking dish, cover with foil and freeze. To serve freezer portion: loosen foil and heat in oven at 425° for 1 hour.

BREAKFAST PIZZA

Debbie Hagood

1 pkg. crescent rolls
1 lb. pork sausage, browned and drained
1 cup frozen shredded hash brown potatoes
1 cup cheddar cheese, shredded
5 eggs
¼ cup milk
¼ tsp. salt
½ tsp. pepper

Spray a 9 x 13 baking pan with baking spray. Roll out crescent roll dough to cover bottom of dish. Add sausage, potatoes and cheese. Beat eggs with milk, salt and pepper. Pour over top. Bake at 375° for 35 minutes.

64809B-05

BRISKET

Mike Feigelson
Peggy Roth

1 first-cut brisket	salt
1 to 2 diced onions	pepper
2 beef bouillon cubes	parsley
½ cup water	dill weed (lots)

Sear brisket in hot 450° oven for 15 minutes on each side. With fat side up, add water, bouillon cubes and seasonings; spread onions over top. Cover and cook in 325° oven for 1½ hours. Add carrots and potatoes; cover and cook another ½ hour. Uncover and cook another ½ hour just to brown. Add water if needed, but do not cover meat in water.

BROILED CHILEAN SEA BASS WITH SMASHED CAULIFLOWER

Laverne and Allen Hoffman

4 pcs. Chilean sea bass (6 to 8-oz. each)	salt and pepper to taste
1 T. honey	1 sm. onion diced and sautéed in olive oil
4 tsp. soy sauce	2 to 3 T. fat free butter
1 head cauliflower, cut into flowerets	2 to 3 T. fat free half and half

Makes 4 servings. Fish: wash and pat dry. Set in glass casserole dish. Drizzle honey on both sides of fish. Spoon 1 teaspoon of soy sauce over each piece of fish. Cover with plastic wrap and marinate at least 1 to 2 hours, turning several times. Preheat broiler to 500°. Remove plastic. Leave fish in casserole and place under broiler for 10 to 12 minutes. This should be wonderfully flaky when a fork is inserted. Place on a bed of mashed cauliflower. Sprinkle a little marinade on top of fish.

Cauliflower

Boil cauliflower till very tender. Drain well in strainer. Mash cauliflower with folk in strainer so excess water can drain. Then place paper towels over cauliflower and press to absorb any additional water. This should be fairly dry. Add butter, half and half, salt and pepper. This may be prepared ahead of time then microwave 1 to 2 minutes before serving.

64809B-05

CAVITINI

Jane Miller, Winship Volunteer

1½ to 2 lbs. seasoned pork
  sausage
1 sm. jar mushrooms
½ cup green pepper, chopped
salt and oregano to taste

1 jar spaghetti sauce
1 can pizza sauce
3 cups cooked curly noodles
1 med. size pkg. mozzarella
  cheese, grated

Makes 4 servings. Pan fry sausage with green pepper, onion and mushrooms. Drain off excess grease. Add cooked noodles and macaroni, tomato sauce and pizza sauce. Season with salt and oregano to taste. Alternate layers in casserole dish, ending with cheese on top. Bake at 350° for approximately 45 minutes. Complete the meal with a tossed green salad and warm garlic bread.

CHEESE BISCUIT SKILLET

Pat Lemeshka, Winship Volunteer

(10-oz.) Hungry Jack Flaky
  Biscuits
(3-oz.) pkg. cream cheese
  softened
½ (2-oz.) cup shredded sharp
  cheese

(10¾-oz.) can cream of
  mushroom soup
3 T. dry onion soup
3 lb. ground beef
1 cup shredded Swiss cheese
2 eggs beaten

Makes 6 servings. Preheat oven to 375°. Separate biscuit dough into 10 biscuits. Press or roll each to a 4-inch circle. Combine cream cheese, ½ cup cheddar cheese and 1 tablespoon of onion soup; blend well. Spoon out 1 tablespoon cream cheese mixture onto center of each biscuit. Fold dough in half over filling. Press edges with fork to seal. In 10-inch ovenproof fry pan, brown ground beef with remaining 2 tablespoons of onion soup mix. Drain. Stir in soup, 1 cup Swiss cheese and eggs. Heat until bubbly. Arrange filled biscuits on hot meat mix. Bake 22 to 28 minutes until deep golden brown.

My joy is contagious.

64809B-05

CHICKEN CACCIATORE

Dorothy Ford

2 to 3 lbs. chicken cut into pieces, or use 1 lb. boneless/skinless chicken pieces
flour
1/4 cup vegetable oil
1 cup celery, sliced
2 med. onions, sliced
2 cloves garlic, minced
1 (16-oz.) can peeled tomatoes

2 (8-oz.) cans tomato sauce
2 chicken bouillon cubes
1 T. sugar
1 tsp. dried basil
1 tsp. salt
1/4 tsp. pepper
1/4 cup water
2 T. cornstarch
Spaghetti, cooked and drained

Makes 4 to 6 servings. Coat chicken with flour and brown in oil. Remove from pan. Add celery, onion and garlic. Cook until tender. Blend in tomatoes, tomato sauce, bouillon and seasonings. Add chicken; cover and simmer about 45 minutes. Blend cornstarch with water and add to chicken; cook until thickened. Arrange on a hot serving dish over spaghetti.

CHICKEN ITALIANO

Jeri Herron

1 chicken cut into small pieces
1/2 green pepper, sliced in strips
2 tsp. oregano
1 pinch sugar
salt and pepper to taste

1 lg. jar of spaghetti sauce
2 cloves garlic, crushed
1 tsp. Italian Seasoning
1 lb. pasta (spaghetti or ziti)

Makes 6 to 8 servings. Wash and season chicken pieces with salt, pepper and garlic. Spray large frying pan or heavy stock pot with oil. Add chicken to heated pot. Lightly brown chicken on all sides, then add spaghetti sauce to the pan. Add the oregano, Italian seasoning and remaining garlic. Reduce heat allowing the chicken to simmer and cook through. Turn chicken until all sides are done--this should take a little over an hour. Serve over pasta that has been boiled according to the box instructions then drained. This dish served on a large platter, garnished with parsley works well for a small dinner party. Serve with a garden salad and Italian/garlic bread.

64809B-05

CHICKEN PARISIENNE

Mary Leigh Harper

6 med. boneless chicken
 breasts
½ cup chicken broth (or dry
 white wine)
1 (10-oz.) can cream of
 mushroom soup

½ cup mushrooms, sliced
 (optional)
paprika
hot cooked rice
½ cup sour cream mixed with
 ¼ cup flour

Makes 4 to 6 servings. Sprinkle chicken breasts with salt and pepper in crockpot. Mix chicken broth, soup and mushrooms until well combined. Pour over chicken breasts in crockpot. Sprinkle with paprika and pepper to taste. Cover and cook on low about 7 hours or high 3 to 4 hours. During last 30 minutes, remove chicken and stir in sour cream mixture. Serve sauce over chicken with rice.

CHICKEN TETRAZZINI

Debbie Foster, Winship Volunteer

1¼ to 1½ cups spaghetti
 broken into 2 inch pieces
1½ to 2 cups cubed cooked
 chicken or turkey
¼ cup diced pimento
¼ cup chopped green pepper
½ chopped small onion

1 can cream of mushroom soup
½ cup chicken broth or water
½ tsp. salt
⅛ tsp. pepper
1¾ cups grated sharp cheese
 (about ½ lb)

Makes 4 to 6 servings. Cook spaghetti and drain. Place chicken, pimento, peppers and onion in 1½-quart casserole dish. Pour in mushroom soup and broth. Add everything else, but set aside ½ cup of cheese to sprinkle on the top. With 2 forks, toss the ingredients until coated. Sprinkle the remaining cheese on top and chill several hours. Bake at 350° for about 45 minutes. To double recipe, use a 3-quart casserole dish, and cook for 1 hour.

64809B-05

CHILI BEAN NACHO SKILLET

Judy Baker
"Taste of Home's: Quick Cooking" November/December
2004

1 lb. ground beef
½ cup chopped onion
1 (15½-oz.) can chili beans,
  undrained
1 (15-oz.) can tomato sauce
1 (11-oz.) can Mexicorn, drained

1 tsp. sugar
1 tsp. chili powder
½ tsp. dried oregano
½ to 1 cup shredded cheddar
  cheese
tortilla chips, optional

Makes 6 servings. In a large skillet, cook beef and onion over medium heat until meat is no longer pink; drain. Stir in the beans, tomato sauce, corn, sugar, chili powder and oregano. Bring to a boil. Reduce heat; simmer, uncovered, for 10 minutes. Sprinkle with cheese; remove from the heat. Cover; let stand for 5 minutes or until cheese is melted. Serve with tortilla chips if desired.

CLASSIC BEEF STROGANOFF

Jane Miller, Winship Volunteer

1 lb. beef tenderloin or sirloin
  steak about ½-inch thick or
  stewing meat
2 T. butter or margarine
½ lb. mushrooms, washed,
  trimmed, and sliced
1 med. onion, minced, about ½
  cup
1 (10½-oz.) can condensed beef
  broth

3 T. flour
2 T. catsup
1 sm. garlic clove, minced
  (garlic salt will do in a pinch)
1 tsp. salt
1 cup sour cream
3 to 4 cups hot cooked noodles

Makes 4 servings. Cut meat across the grain into ½-inch strips, about 1½-inch long. Melt butter in large skillet. Add mushrooms and onion. Cook and stir until light brown. Reserving ⅓ cup of broth, stir in remaining broth, catsup, garlic and salt. Cover; simmer 15 minutes. Blend reserved broth and flour; stir into meat mixture. Add mushrooms and onion. Heat to boiling, stirring constantly. Boil and stir 1 minute. Reduce heat. Stir in sour cream. Heat. Serve over noodles.

64809B-05

EASY LASAGNA

Debbie Merk

1 (9-oz.) box oven ready lasagna noodles (uncooked)
2 eggs
1 (15-oz.) container ricotta cheese
4 cups (10-oz.) of shredded mozzarella cheese

½ cup (2-oz.) Parmesan cheese (optional)
1 lb. Italian sausage (cook, crumble, drain)
2 (26-oz.) jars of your favorite baking sauce, spaghetti or marinara sauce

Makes 12 servings. Preheat oven to 375°. Spray lasagna baking pan (13 x 9 x 3 deep) with nonstick cooking spray. In medium bowl mix ricotta, 2 cups mozzarella and Parmesan. Layer uncooked lasagna noodles slightly overlapping pieces. Spread fillings to edges to seal in and cook lasagna during baking. Layer in the following order: spread one cup of sauce on bottom of baking pan. Layer 4 uncooked noodles, ⅓ ricotta mixture, half of browned meat, 1 cup mozzarella; top with 1 cup sauce. Layer 4 uncooked noodles, ⅓ ricotta mixture and 1½ cups sauce. Layer 4 uncooked noodles, remaining ricotta mixture, browned meat and 1 cup sauce. Layer 4 uncooked noodles and remaining sauce. Bake covered with foil until bubbly--50 to 60 minutes. Uncover and top with 1 cup mozzarella cheese and continue to cook until cheese is melted. Let stand 15 minutes before cutting. For a lower fat version, use ground pork and add your own Italian seasonings (oregano, basil, or hot pepper flakes).

EASY PARMESAN GARLIC CHICKEN

Sarah Wilson

½ cup grated Parmesan cheese
1 pkg. Italian Dressing Mix (for zing try Zesty Italian Mix)

½ tsp. garlic powder
4 boneless skinless chicken breast halves

Mix first 3 ingredients. Moisten the chicken with water; coat with cheese mixture. Place in a shallow baking dish. Bake at 400° for 20 to 25 minutes until done.

When difficulties arise, I remain positive.

64809B-05

FAMILY FLANK STEAK

Judy Baker
"Taste of Home's: Quick Cooking" November/December
2004

1 beef flank steak (1 lb)
1 T. canola oil
¼ cup red wine or beef broth

Mushroom Wine Sauce

1 cup sliced fresh mushrooms
¾ cup beef broth
¼ cup red wine or additional
   beef broth
¼ cup chopped green onions

1 T. Worcestershire sauce
1 tsp. minced fresh basil or ½
   tsp. dried basil

1 tsp. butter
1 tsp. pepper
2 tsp. cornstarch
1 T. cold water

Makes 4 servings. In a large skillet, brown steak in oil. Stir in the wine or broth, Worcestershire sauce and basil. Bring to a boil. Reduce heat; simmer, uncovered, for 2 to 4 minutes on each side or until meat reaches desired doneness (for rare, a meat thermometer should read 140°; medium 160°; well-done 170°). Remove steak and keep warm. To the skillet, add mushrooms, broth, wine or additional broth, onions, butter and pepper. Bring to a boil. Reduce heat; simmer, uncovered, for 5 minutes or until mushrooms are tender. Combine cornstarch and water until smooth; stir into sauce. Bring to a boil; cook and stir for 1 minute or until thickened. Thinly slice steak across the grain; serve with sauce.

GLAZED HAM

Judy Baker
Interpreted from "Good Housekeeping: A Very Merry
Christmas Cookbook 2003"

1 14 lb. fully cooked smoked
   whole ham
½ cup apple jelly

¼ tsp. ground ginger
fresh herbs for garnish

Makes 20 main dish servings. Preheat oven to 325°. Remove skin and trim some fat from ham, leaving about ¼-inch fat covering. Place ham on rack in large roasting pan (17 x 11½). Bake ham 2 hours 30 minutes. Then prepare glaze: In small saucepan, combine apple jelly and ginger and heat to boiling over medium-high heat; boil 2 minutes. Brush ham with some glaze. Bake ham 30 minutes to 1 hour longer, brushing occasionally with remaining glaze--until a meat thermometer inserted into center of ham registers 140° (15 to 18 minutes per pound total cooking time). When ham is done, transfer to warm large platter; let stand 20 minutes to set juices for easier slicing. Garnish with herbs.

64809B-05

GREEK STEAK PITAS WITH DILL SAUCE
Andrea Roberts

1 lb. flank steak
Pitas

Sauce

½ cup plain yogurt
2 tsp. chopped fresh dill
¼ tsp. salt

Marinade

½ cup fresh lemon juice
1 tsp. dried oregano

Romaine Lettuce
Feta Cheese

¼ tsp. black pepper
1 garlic clove, minced

½ tsp. black pepper
2 garlic cloves, minced

Makes 4 servings. Marinate the steak in a zip-lock bag for 10 minutes, turning once. Remove steak and discard marinade. Grill steak until done (6 minutes per side), cut steak into bite size pieces. Make sauce while steak is on the grill. Serve in pitas with lettuce, yogurt sauce and feta cheese.

GREEK STYLE SCAMPI
Robert and Eve Willson
Original source: Cooking Light

1 tsp. olive oil
5 garlic cloves, minced
½ cup chopped fresh parsley, divided
2 (28-oz.) cans whole tomatoes, drained and coarsely chopped
1¼ lb. lg. shrimp, peeled and deveined

1 (4-oz.) cup crumbled feta cheese
2 T. fresh lemon juice
¼ tsp. freshly ground black pepper
4 cups hot cooked spaghetti (about 8-oz. uncooked pasta)

Makes 6 servings. Preheat oven to 400°. Heat oil in a large Dutch oven over medium heat. Add garlic; sauté for 30 seconds. Add ¼ cup parsley and tomatoes. Reduce heat; simmer for 10 minutes. Add shrimp; cook for 5 minutes. Pour mixture into a 9 x 13 baking dish. Sprinkle with cheese. Bake at 400° for 10 minutes. Sprinkle with ¼ cup parsley, lemon juice and pepper. Serve over pasta.

64809B-05

GRILLED PORK TENDERLOIN

Jeannie Wright, Winship Volunteer

2 pork tenderloins

Marinade

½ cup Dijon mustard
1 clove garlic, minced
¼ cup olive oil
3 T. white wine

½ tsp. thyme
½ tsp. ground black pepper
1 tsp. Worcestershire sauce

Makes 6 servings. Combine all marinade ingredients in a bowl with a wire whisk until well blended. Coat meat thoroughly. Put in plastic bag and let stand at room temperature for 30 minutes or in the refrigerator for 4 to 6 hours. Grill over medium hot fire, approximately 20 minutes on each side. Baste frequently with marinade while cooking.

HEARTY CHICKEN BAKE

Elaine Koenig

3 cups hot mashed potatoes
1 cup shredded cheddar cheese
1 (2.8-oz.) can French's French Fried Onions
1½ cups cubed cooked chicken
1 (10-oz.) pkg. frozen mixed vegetables, thawed and drained

1 (10¼-oz.) can condensed cream of chicken soup
¼ cup milk
½ tsp. ground mustard
¼ tsp. garlic powder
¼ tsp. pepper

Makes 4 to 6 servings. Preheat oven to 375°. In a medium bowl, combine mashed potatoes, ½ cup cheese and ½ can French Fried Onions; mix thoroughly. Spoon potato mixture into greased 1½-quart casserole dish. Using back of spoon, spread potatoes across bottom and up sides of dish to form a shell. In a large bowl, combine chicken, mixed vegetables, soup, milk and seasonings; pour into potato shell. Bake uncovered at 375° for 30 minutes or until heated through. Top with remaining cheese and onions; bake uncovered for 3 minutes or until onions are golden brown. Let stand for 5 minutes and serve.

64809B-05

HONEY CHICKEN

Mary Leigh Harper

¼ cup flour
½ tsp. salt
4 boneless chicken breasts
½ cup butter, melted

½ cup honey
¼ cup lemon juice
1 tsp. soy sauce

Makes 4 servings. Preheat oven to 350°. Dip chicken in flour and salt mixture. Arrange in a baking dish. Pour butter over chicken and bake 30 minutes. Mix the rest of the ingredients; pour over chicken, bake 30 minutes--basting often.

ISLAND SPICE SALMON

Sally Hopkins
Original source: "Light and Tasty" magazine, sent
by Kathryn Samodell

2 T. brown sugar
2 T. chili powder
2 tsp. ground cumin

1 tsp. salt
½ tsp. ground cinnamon
1 salmon filet (2 lbs)

Makes 8 servings. In a small bowl, combine the first 5 ingredients; mix well. Rub over flesh side of filet. Refrigerate for 30 minutes, skin side down, in a 13 x 9 x 2 baking dish coated with non-stick cooking spray. Bake at 375° for 20 to 25 minutes until fish flakes easily with a fork. Chicken or pork may be substituted for salmon.

LASAGNA

Pat Sachs

1 lb. ground beef
¾ cup onion chopped
1 (16-oz.) can chopped tomatoes
1 (16-oz.) can tomato paste
½ cup water
1 garlic clove, minced
1 tsp. oregano

¼ tsp. pepper
1 lb. cooked lasagna noodles
2 (6-oz.) pkgs. sliced mozzarella
  cheese
½ lb. Velveeta, sliced
½ cup Parmesan cheese

Makes 6 to 8 servings. Brown hamburger and onion in a large skillet. Add tomatoes, water, tomato paste and spices. Simmer 20 minutes. Boil noodles according to package directions. Alternately layer noodles, meat sauce and sliced cheeses. Sprinkle Parmesan on top. Bake at 350° for 30 minutes or until hot and bubbly.

64809B-05

MANDARIN ORANGE CHICKEN

Judy Baker
"Taste of Home's: Quick Cooking" November/December
2004

4 (4-oz.) boneless/skinless
chicken breast halves
2 T. all-purpose flour
¼ tsp. salt
¼ tsp. pepper
1 T. canola oil
½ cup orange juice

¼ cup orange marmalade
2 T. honey mustard
¼ tsp. dried rosemary, crushed
1 (11-oz.) can mandarin
oranges, drained
1 tsp. grated orange peel
hot cooked rice, optional

Makes 4 servings. Flatten chicken to ¼-inch thickness. In a shallow dish, combine the flour, salt and pepper; coat chicken. In a large skillet, brown chicken in oil on both sides. Combine orange juice, marmalade, mustard and rosemary; pour over chicken. Bring to a boil; cook for 5 to 8 minutes or until chicken juices run clear and sauce is thickened. Stir in oranges and orange peel. Serve over rice if desired.

MAPLE-APPLE PORK SLICES

Judy Baker
"Taste of Home's: Quick Cooking" November/December
2004

1 lb. pork tenderloin, cut into
¼-inch slices
¼ cup seasoned bread crumbs
2 T. olive oil
2 med. tart apples, peeled and
sliced

½ cup apple juice or cider
¼ cup maple syrup
1 T. prepared mustard
¼ tsp. salt
¼ tsp. pepper

Makes 4 servings. Coat pork slices with bread crumbs. In a large skillet, cook pork in oil over medium-high heat for 2 minutes on each side. Add the apples and juice; cover and cook for 10 minutes or until apples are tender. Combine the syrup, mustard, salt and pepper; pour over pork mixture. Cook, uncovered, for 2 minutes or until heated through.

When difficulties arise, I remain positive.

64809B-05

MEAT LOAF

Barbara Faro

1½ lbs. ground beef
1½ cups bread crumbs
2 eggs
1 (8-oz.) cup tomato sauce
½ cup chopped onion

2 T. chopped green pepper
1½ tsp. salt
1 dash thyme
1 dash marjoram

Makes 4 servings. Mix together and shape into loaf and bake in loaf pan 1 hour at 350°.

MEAT LOAF FLORENTINE

Nin Sciretta, Winship Volunteer

1 egg, slightly beaten
1½ cups bread crumbs (2 slices bread)
1 cup milk
2 lbs. ground beef

1¼ tsp. salt
2 T. soy sauce
1 (10-oz.) pkg. chopped spinach thawed and drained

Mix all the meat loaf ingredients and bake at 350° for 1¼ hours.

Mushroom sauce

1 (32-oz.) can sliced mushroom undrained
2 T. flour

1 cup sour cream
2 T. chives

Stir all ingredients until it thickens; do not boil. The mushroom sauce can be used in place of ketchup.

64809B-05

MEAT LOAF WITH SUN-DRIED TOMATOES AND HERBS

Linda Appleton

Meat Loaf

1 med. onion, finely chopped
1 bell pepper, finely chopped
1 T. extra virgin olive oil
1 lb. ground round
(2-oz.) sun-dried tomatoes, rehydrated, drained, finely chopped
(6-oz.) provolone or mozzarella cheese, shredded
2 lg. eggs, beaten

2 cloves garlic, minced
1 slice bread, softened in ⅛ cup milk, drained
2 tsp. dried basil
1 tsp. salt
1 tsp. dried oregano
1 tsp. dried thyme
1 tsp. freshly ground black pepper

Makes 6 servings. In microwave, soften onion and bell pepper in olive oil on high for 2 minutes, and cool. Preheat oven to 350°. Combine onion, bell pepper, ground round, tomatoes, cheese, eggs, garlic, bread, basil, salt, oregano, thyme and pepper. Press meat loaf mixture into lightly greased 5 x 9½ loaf pan. Bake 1 hour, pouring off fat as necessary and reserving drippings for gravy, if desired.

Sun-dried Tomato Gravy

¼ cup drippings from meat loaf
1 T. all-purpose flour
½ pt. half & half
(½-oz.) sun-dried tomatoes, rehydrated, drained, finely chopped

1 T. finely chopped green onion
1 T. chopped fresh basil (1 tsp. dried)
salt and pepper to taste

Whisk drippings with flour over medium heat. Whisk in half & half and stir to thicken. Add tomatoes, green onion, basil, salt and pepper; heat thoroughly. Serve gravy over sliced meat loaf.

64809B-05

MEDITERRANEAN CHICKEN

Tiffany Barrett

4 tsp. chopped garlic
1 T. olive oil
1 tsp. salt
1 tsp. black pepper
12 red potatoes, quartered
2 lbs. skinless, boneless
  chicken breasts cut into pieces
1 cup sliced onion

1 cup reduced fat, low sodium
  chicken broth
½ cup white wine (may
  substitute sherry)
2 cups chopped tomatoes
2 T. chopped fresh basil
1 can artichoke hearts,
  quartered and drained

Preheat oven to 400°. Combine 2 teaspoons garlic, oil, ¼ teaspoon salt, ¼ teaspoon pepper and potatoes in a pan. Bake the potatoes in the 400° oven for 30 minutes. Heat a large Dutch oven coated with cooking spray over medium-high heat. Sprinkle chicken with ½ teaspoon salt and ¼ teaspoon pepper. Add chicken to pan; sauté 5 to 6 minutes. Remove chicken. Add onion to pan; cook 5 minutes. Add wine and bring to a boil; cook for 2 minutes. Add potatoes, chicken and broth; cook 4 minutes. Stir in 2 teaspoons of garlic, ¼ teaspoon salt, tomatoes, basil and artichokes. Cook 4 minutes.

MEDITERRANEAN-STYLE BEEF TURNOVERS

Stella Kazazian, Winship Volunteer

1 lb. lean ground beef
1 med. onion, finely chopped
2½ T. butter
1 tsp. cinnamon
1 tsp. dried basil
1 tsp. salt
½ tsp. freshly ground black
  pepper

1 T. tomato paste
½ cup pine nuts, slightly
  toasted
2 to 3 pkgs. refrigerated biscuit
  dough
¼ cup sour cream or plain
  yogurt

Preheat oven to 375°. In a large frying pan, sauté onion in butter, until soft. Remove onions from pan; add ground beef to pan and brown. Drain off oil. Add onions back to pan. Add tomato paste, salt, pepper, basil, cinnamon and pine nuts to pan. Mix well. Slowly add enough sour cream or yogurt to hold mixture together. Set aside to cool. Open 1 package of biscuits at a time, remove biscuits. With fingers or rolling pin, flatten each to a 3 to 4-inch round. Place 2 to 2½ teaspoons of meat mixture on one side. Fold other side over the mixture; with a fork dipped in flour, crimp the edges to close. Continue until all are done. Bake until turnovers are golden brown. Serve warm with a Greek or Italian style salad.

64809B-05

MEXICAN WHITE CHILI

Barry Rabinowitch

1 lg. onion, diced
1 lg. green pepper, medium dice
½ red pepper, medium dice
2 sm. jalapeño pepper, small dice
3 cloves garlic, minced
3 T. olive oil
3 (14-oz.) cans chicken broth or 42-oz. can chicken soup

3 chicken bouillon cubes
3 cups diced chicken
1 (14-oz.) can white navy beans
½ cup chopped fresh cilantro or 2 tablespoons dried cilantro
¼ tsp. black pepper
(10-oz.) tortilla chips
(8-oz.) grated cheddar cheese

Sauté first 6 ingredients in a 3 to 5-quart soup pot until onions are tender. Add chicken broth to sautéed vegetables and dissolve bouillon cubes. Simmer for 15 minutes. In a food processor, work 10 ounces of tortilla chips to fine crumbs and add to simmering broth. Continue to simmer and stir until mixture is thickened. Rinse white beans and drain, then add to mixture with cilantro and black pepper. Add diced chicken and heat for another minute before serving. Sprinkle with grated cheese as desired.

PARMESAN PEPPER MEATBALLS

Florence Greeson

1 lb. ground beef
Parmesan cheese
½ cup dry bread crumbs
2 eggs
½ tsp. garlic powder
½ tsp. salt
all-purpose oil
3 cups water

2 beef bouillon cubes
½ cup celery slices
2 T. cornstarch
½ cup green pepper strips
½ cup onion slices
1 cup mushroom slices
¼ cup pimento strips
hot cooked noodles

Makes 4 to 6 servings. Combine meat, ½ cup cheese, bread crumbs, eggs and seasonings. Shape into 18 balls. Brown in oil; drain. Add 1½ cups water, bouillon cubes and celery. Cover; simmer 10 minutes. Combine cornstarch and remaining 1½ cups water, stirring constantly until well blended. Gradually add cornstarch mixture to meatballs, stirring until it boils and thickens. Add remaining vegetables. Cover; simmer 5 minutes, stirring occasionally. Serve over noodles.

64809B-05

PASTA E FAGIOLI

Angela Fortezza-Soto

2 tsp. olive oil
3 cloves garlic, minced or
  smashed
water
1 can cannellini beans, drained

ditalini or medium shell pasta
2 tsp. oregano (or one of those
  mixes of Italian herbs)
salt and pepper to taste

Makes 2 to 4 servings. Heat olive oil in a small saucepan; cook garlic for a couple of minutes taking care it doesn't get brown. Add the beans and enough water to cover the beans by about an inch. Add oregano or whatever herbs you are using and let it simmer while the pasta cooks in boiling salted water. When the pasta is done, drain and return to the pot, then dump the beans (and juices) on top of the pasta. Ladle into individual dishes and top with freshly ground pepper and maybe a little drizzle of fresh extra virgin olive oil, if desired. Enjoy!

PORK CHOP SKILLET MEAL

Elaine Scales
Original source: old church cook book

5 pork chop medallions
4 to 6 sliced peeled potatoes
1 can cream of mushroom soup

1 T. oil
½ cup water
1 onion, sliced

Season pork chops and brown on one side in large skillet, then turn them over. Put a layer of sliced onions over chops, then a layer of sliced raw potatoes. Continue with these layers, sprinkling with salt and pepper to taste until pan is almost full, but allowing room to cook. Add ½ cup water to the soup and mix until smooth. Pour over pork chop mixture and cook on medium heat for 1 hour.

Today, I chose to be peaceful.

64809B-05

RED SNAPPER VERACRUZ

Stella Kazazian, Winship Volunteer

2 lbs. red snapper fillets
1 lg. onion, chopped
1 lg. carrot, chopped
1 green pepper, seeded and
chopped
2 lg. ripe tomatoes, cut up and
try to save the juice
1 tsp. finely minced garlic
1/4 cup lime juice

1 tsp. chili powder
2 T. cilantro, coarsely chopped
1 to 2 tsp. salt
1/2 tsp. fresh cracked black
pepper
3 T. olive or vegetable oil
pitted green or black olives,
sliced (optional for garnish)

In a large frying pan, on medium-low heat, sauté the onions, carrot and green pepper until soft. Add the tomatoes, garlic, lime juice, chili powder, cilantro, salt and pepper. Continue cooking for 5 minutes. Place fish fillets into sauce; cook until fish is done.

NOTE: 1. You may place sauce in a greased baking dish, then place fish in sauce. Bake in a 350° oven for 10 minutes or until fish is cooked. 2. Chicken breasts may be substituted for fish fillets.

SHANNON'S CHICKEN

Claire Smith

6 to 8 chicken breast fillets
1 bottle Zesty Italian salad
dressing

garlic powder to taste

Place chicken in an oven proof dish. Pour dressing over chicken and sprinkle with garlic powder. Marinate for 1 hour or overnight. Bake at 350° for 30 minutes.

64809B-05

SHRIMP PASTA

Carmen Wynn

1 jar classic Alfredo (Ragu) sauce
1 stick Land O' Lakes sweet cream butter
½ cup minced garlic

1 bag (50 to 70) medium frozen shrimp
salt and pepper to taste
garlic salt to taste
1 box linguini noodles

Makes 4 servings. Boil noodles--follow instructions on box. Sauté shrimp with butter and garlic for about 5 minutes on high. Lower heat to medium low; add Alfredo sauce. Stir; add salt, pepper, and garlic salt to taste. Stir when noodles are done. Pour sauce over noodles and enjoy. For a party of 8, double ingredients.

SHRIMP PRIMAVERA

Judith Bahc

lg. jar primavera pasta sauce
3 yellow squash, sliced
3 med. zucchini, sliced
6 asparagus stalks (cut in 2 inch pieces)

8 med. mushrooms, sliced
1½ lbs. cooked, peeled shrimp
1 lb. linguini
shredded Parmesan cheese

Makes 4 to 6 servings. Sauté all vegetables in pasta sauce until tender. Add shrimp just before serving to heat (not cook). Cook linguini until tender. Drain. Serve sauce over linguini.

SLOPPY JOES

Kathy Fonder

1 lb. hamburger
1 onion, chopped fine
2 to 3 stalks celery, chopped fine
1 T. prepared mustard

1 T. Worcestershire sauce
½ cup catsup
1 can tomato soup
½ - ¾ can water
salt and pepper to taste

Brown hamburger and drain. Mix with browned onion and celery. Add mustard, Worcestershire sauce, catsup, soup and water. Add salt and pepper to taste. Simmer 1 hour. Stir occasionally. Serve over hamburger buns.

64809B-05

SOUR CREAM ENCHILADAS

Susan E. Ottinger
Original source: Susan A. Ottinger

1 can cream of chicken soup
½ to 1 cup sour cream
2 T. butter or margarine
½ cup chopped onions
1 (4-oz.) can green chiles
1 tsp. chili powder

2 cups diced, cooked chicken
breast
8 flour tortillas
1 to 2 cups grated cheese
(Monterey Jack, Cheddar, or
both)

Makes 6 to 8 servings. Preheat oven to 375°. Stir soup and sour cream until smooth. In a 2-quart saucepan over medium heat, in hot butter; cook onion and chili powder until onion is tender. Stir in chicken and 2 tablespoons of soup mixture. Add chiles. Fill each tortilla with chicken mixture, sprinkle with cheese, roll up and place in a 9 x 13 dish. Pour soup mixture over enchiladas and sprinkle remaining cheese on top. Cover with foil and bake 15 minutes. Remove foil and bake 5 minutes uncovered.

SPICY PORK TENDERLOIN

Stella Kazazian, Winship Volunteer

½ cup red wine
½ cup water
1 onion, peeled and sliced
2 T. chopped scallions or
shallots
½ tsp. cinnamon
1 sm. bay leaf
1 whole clove
3 sprigs parsley
½ tsp. thyme

⅛ tsp. salt
pepper to taste
2 lbs. pork tenderloin, cut into
½ inch slices
3 T. butter and oil
2 T. flour
½ cup chicken stock or broth
2 T. brandy (optional, can use
brandy flavoring)

Makes 6 to 8 servings. Preheat oven to 375°. In a bowl, combine wine, water, onion, shallots, cinnamon, bay leaf, clove, parsley, thyme, salt and pepper. Arrange meat slices in 1 layer in a shallow dish and pour marinade over it, turning to moisten. Marinate 2 hours, turning once. Remove meat from marinade and reserve marinade. Heat butter and oil in a large skillet and brown meat, 2 to 3 minutes per side. Transfer to baking dish. Add flour to fat in skillet and cook on low heat, mixing until flour is lightly browned. Pour in strained marinade, chicken stock and brandy. Stir constantly with wire whisk and bring to a boil. Continue whisking until sauce is smooth and slightly thickened. Taste for seasoning. Pour sauce over meat and bake for 5 minutes.

64809B-05

SPINACH PORK TENDERLOIN

Judy Baker
"Taste of Home's: Quick Cooking" November/December
2004

2 cups torn fresh spinach
¼ cup water
½ cup frozen artichoke hearts, thawed and chopped
⅓ cup shredded Parmesan cheese

¼ tsp. dried rosemary, crushed
1 pork tenderloin (1 lb)
½ tsp. salt, divided
⅛ tsp. pepper

Sauce

½ cup apple-cranberry juice concentrate

¼ cup balsamic vinegar
1 T. sugar

Makes 4 servings. In a nonstick skillet, cook the spinach and water over medium heat for 3 to 4 minutes or until wilted; drain well. Combine the spinach, artichokes, Parmesan cheese and rosemary; set aside. Cut a lengthwise slit down center of tenderloin to within ½-inch of bottom. Open meat so it lies flat; cover with plastic wrap. Flatten to ¼-inch thickness; remove plastic. Sprinkle meat with ¼ teaspoon salt; top with spinach mixture. Close meat; tie with kitchen strings and secure ends with toothpicks. Sprinkle with pepper and remaining salt. Place in a shallow baking pan. Bake at 425° for 15 minutes. Meanwhile, in a small saucepan, combine the sauce ingredients. Bring to a boil over medium heat. Reduce heat; simmer, uncovered, for 15 minutes. Pour over the meat. Bake 10 minutes longer or until a meat thermometer reads 160°. Let stand for 10 minutes before slicing.

I expect good things to happen in my life.

64809B-05

SPINACH TOFU QUICHE

Tiffany Barrett

1½ cup chopped onion
1 cup sliced mushrooms
2 tsp. garlic
3 T. olive oil
(16-oz.) soft tofu
(10-oz.) pkg. chopped frozen
spinach, thawed and drained

1 T. lemon juice
1 tsp. salt
2 T. dill seeds
¼ cup Feta cheese, crumbled
¼ cup shredded Parmesan
cheese
1 partially baked pie shell

Makes 6 servings. Preheat oven to 400°. Sauté onions, mushrooms and garlic in 1 tablespoon olive oil, over low heat, until soft. Add spinach, lemon juice, salt and dill seeds; heat. In a blender, combine tofu and 2 tablespoons olive oil; blend until smooth. Add to spinach mixture with Feta cheese. Pour into pie crust and bake for 30 minutes or until set. Sprinkle with Parmesan cheese and let stand for about 10 minutes.

SPINACH, GARLIC, AND CHICKEN PASTA

Mary Booth Thomas, Winship Volunteer

1½ heads garlic, peeled
2 cups cold water
3 red, yellow or orange bell
peppers or combination
½ pkg. fresh spinach
2 tsp. chopped fresh thyme
1 can white beans, rinsed and
drained

1 T. Balsamic vinegar
1 T. extra-virgin olive oil
2 cooked chicken breasts, diced
(10-oz.) penne pasta
½ cup Parmesan cheese

Put all but six large garlic cloves in cold water and simmer until garlic is very soft--about 30 minutes. Purée garlic in ½ cup of the garlic cooking liquid with 1 teaspoon of salt in a blender until smooth. Roast peppers on gas burner or in broiler pan until skins are black. Transfer to a bowl and cover with plastic wrap until cool. Peel peppers and cut into ¼-inch pieces. Mince 2 of the reserved garlic cloves with thyme and 1 teaspoon of salt. Put spinach and garlic-thyme mixture in a large serving bowl. Chop remaining garlic clove and cook in olive oil until pale golden, 3 to 5 minutes. Add chicken and peppers and cook for 5 minutes, stirring often. Add beans and garlic purée and bring to a simmer over low heat. Meanwhile, cook and drain pasta. Add pasta, chicken mixture, sauce, vinegar and cheese to spinach. Mix and serve immediately.

64809B-05

STICKY CHICKEN

Caryn Shulman

4 to 6 boneless chicken breasts without the skin
1 sm. bottle of fat free Catalina dressing

1 pkg. Uptons onion soup mix
1/2 jar peach preserves

Makes 4 to 6 servings. Place chicken breasts in baking pan. Mix together salad dressing, onion soup mix and peach preserves. Pour over chicken. Bake at 375° for 30 minutes covered. Uncover chicken, baste with sauce and bake uncovered for 15 minutes. Serve with rice.

STIR FRY SHRIMP

Debbie Foster, Winship Volunteer

1 clove garlic or 1/4 T. minced
1 T. fresh ginger, grated
3 T. olive oil
1 lb. cleaned shrimp
1/2 lb. snow pea pods or 1 frozen pkg. of snow peas

1 T. cornstarch
2 T. soy sauce
2 T. dry sherry
1/2 cup chicken broth

Makes 3 to 4 servings. Sauté garlic and ginger in oil. Add cleaned shrimp for 1 minute. Add pea pods for 2 minutes (if using frozen snow peas, you may need to adjust their cooking time accordingly). Mix last ingredients and add to shrimp and pods to thicken slightly. Serve over rice.

STUFFED MUSHROOMS

Barbara Faro

1 lb. sausage cooked and drained
1 (8-oz.) pkg. cream cheese

mushrooms
bread crumbs
Parmesan cheese

Makes 6 servings. Cook sausage and drain. Mix in cream cheese and small amount of bread crumbs. Remove stems from the washed mushrooms and add to the sausage and cheese; lightly sauté. Stuff in mushroom caps and sprinkle with Parmesan cheese. Bake in the oven at 475° for 15 to 20 minutes.

64809B-05

STUFFED TOMATOES

Catherine Macrenaris

10 lg. tomatoes
2 lbs. lean ground beef
(4-oz.) butter
1 cup diced onions
2 T. mint leaves
1 T. ground cinnamon

1 (8-oz.) can tomato sauce
2 (20-oz.) can tomato sauce
1/2 cup uncooked rice
1 cup raisins
salt and pepper to taste

Makes 10 servings. Slice tops from tomatoes and reserve. Scoop pulp from tomatoes carefully and drain tomatoes. Place tomato shells in large baking dish. Sprinkle shells with salt. Dice the pulp. In a large skillet, sauté onions and add meat; stir until brown. Add 2 cups tomato pulp, raisins, rice, mint, cinnamon, salt, pepper and 8 ounce can of tomato sauce; simmer 10 minutes. Fill tomato shells almost to the top with meat mixture. Replace tops. Pour the 20 ounce can of tomato sauce in the bottom of the pan. Bake in 375° preheated oven for 1 1/2 hours. Baste often.

SWEET 'N' SOUR TURKEY

Judy Baker
"Taste of Home's: Quick Cooking" November/December 2004

2 T. cornstarch
2 T. brown sugar
1 cup chicken broth
2 T. soy sauce
1 T. lemon juice
2 celery ribs, sliced
2 med. carrots, sliced
1 sm. onion, cut into thin
wedges

3 T. butter, cubed
2 cups julienned cooked turkey
1 (14-oz.) can unsweetened
pineapple tidbits, undrained
1/4 cup slivered almonds,
toasted
hot cooked rice, optional

Makes 4 servings. In a small bowl, combine cornstarch and brown sugar. Stir in the broth, soy sauce and lemon juice until smooth; set aside. In a wok or large skillet, stir-fry the celery, carrots and onions in butter for 4 minutes or until crisp-tender. Stir broth mixture; add to the pan. Bring to a boil; cook and stir for 2 minutes or until thickened. Add turkey, pineapple with juice and almonds; heat through. Serve over rice if desired.

64809B-05

TERIYAKI STEAK

Mary Leigh Harper

1 flank steak, approximately 1½ lbs
¼ cup soy sauce
3 T. honey
2 T. vinegar

1 clove garlic, minced
1 tsp. freshly grated ginger
3 green onions, tops included, chopped (optional)
¾ cup vegetable oil

Makes 6 servings. Marinade: In a 2 cup glass measuring cup, combine soy sauce, honey, vinegar, garlic, ginger and onions. Gradually whisk in oil. Pierce steak on both sides with a fork. Place in a baking dish. Pour marinade over steak. Turn several times to coat. Cover. Marinate at cool room temperature or in the refrigerator for approximately 4 hours. Turn steak in marinade once every hour. Barbecue steak outdoors, under a broiler or use an electric grill. Baste periodically with marinade. If you have them, during the last few minutes of cooking, spoon on some of the green onions. If cooking indoors, baste only once to avoid too much smoke. Cut diagonally into 1-inch strips. Cook to desired doneness. This recipe works well with chicken.

TUNA STEAK ON WHITE BEANS WITH TOMATO COULIS

Mary Booth Thomas, Winship Volunteer

1 lb. fresh tuna steaks, preferably sashimi grade
2 cans cannellini (white beans)
2 cloves garlic, minced
fresh rosemary
2 T. olive oil

2 ripe tomatoes or 4-oz. grape tomatoes
3 sprigs fresh basil
Capers
salt
olive oil

Prepare beans: Sauté garlic in olive oil until it starts to turn golden. Drain most of the water from the beans and add to garlic. Add 2 to 3 whole sprigs of rosemary. Cook over medium heat until the beans are mushy. Remove rosemary sprigs. Tomato coulis: Chop tomatoes and basil. Mix with capers. Salt to taste. Sprinkle a little olive oil over the mixture and microwave on high for 30 seconds. Grill or broil tuna steak to desired doneness. Cut into four equal portions. To serve: Put bean purée on plate. Put tuna on top. Top with tomato coulis.

64809B-05

TURKEY SLOPPY JOE

Yasha Hill

ground turkey
tomato paste
Sloppy Joe seasoning

toasted wheat buns
onion (½ of a small) diced

Makes 3 to 4 servings. Cook a pound of ground turkey and ½ of an onion, let it brown. Drain; add seasoning, tomato paste and water. Let it simmer until thick and hearty. Toast wheat buns to your own doneness.

UPSIDE DOWN PIZZA PIE

Lynn Gibson

½ cup canned pizza sauce
1 cup shredded mozzarella
  cheese
1 pkg. sliced pepperoni

1 egg, well beaten
¾ cup milk
¾ cup self-rising flour

Makes 4 servings. Preheat oven to 375°. Spray a 9-inch pie pan with vegetable cooking spray. Spread pizza sauce over bottom of pie plate. Layer pepperoni, then cheese. Mix egg, flour and milk to form a smooth batter. Pour over the cheese. Bake 20 to 25 minutes or until golden brown.

I radiate joy, peace and love.

64809B-05

CASSEROLES

BAKED BLINTZ CASSEROLE

Elaine Koenig

Dough

½ lb. soft butter	3 tsp. baking powder
½ cup sugar	¼ cup milk
2 eggs	1 tsp. vanilla
1 cup flour	

Filling

2 lbs. cottage cheese	2 eggs
juice of 1 lemon	1 tsp. vanilla
¼ cup sugar	(4-oz.) cream cheese

Makes 12 servings. Preheat oven to 300°. Melt butter in 2-quart casserole dish. Combine remaining dough ingredients and mix well. Divide dough in half; put half in the bottom of the casserole dish. Mix filling ingredients in a separate bowl. Add filling to casserole dish. Use the remaining half of dough for the top. Bake 1½ hours at 300° or until brown. Cut into squares and serve with sour cream or strawberry jam. Freezable.

BREAKFAST CASSEROLE

Shirley Whitehead

6 eggs slightly beaten	1 lb. hot sausage cooked,
2 cups milk	drained and crumbled
1 tsp. salt	4 cups sharp cheese grated
1 tsp. dry mustard	
6 slices of white bread, cut into cubes	

Makes 8 to 10 servings. Arrange bread cubes in a 7½ x 11½ baking dish sprayed with cooking spray. Top with sausage and cheese. Combine milk, eggs, salt and mustard. Pour over sausage mixture. Refrigerate overnight. Bake at 350° for 35 minutes. Options: substitute bacon or ham for sausage, and Swiss cheese for cheddar.

64809B-05

BROCCOLI CASSEROLE

Mary Leigh Harper

2 sm. pkgs. frozen chopped
 broccoli
1 can creamy chicken and
 mushroom soup
1 sm. onion, chopped

1 to 2 cups grated cheddar
 cheese
1 egg
1 cup mayonnaise
bread crumbs

Makes 6 servings. Cook broccoli to package directions. Strain broccoli and put in large mixing bowl. Add the rest of the ingredients except bread crumbs. Put mixture in casserole dish and bake at 350° for 25 minutes. Put topping on casserole and bake 10 more minutes.

CHEESY CHICKEN AND RICE CASSEROLE

Nikki Elliott

3 cups cooked rice
1 lb. chicken, diced and cooked

2 cups broccoli, cooked

Makes 4 servings. Put first 3 ingredients in a 9 x 13 pan. Add sauce and mix well. Cook at 350° for 30 minutes or until heated through. Add topping and cook 5 more minutes.

Sauce

1 sm. pkg. Velveeta cheese
1 can cream of chicken soup

4-6 oz. sour cream
2 T. milk

Combine sauce ingredients in a small saucepan. Cook over medium heat, stirring constantly until mixture is smooth.

(Hint: you may want to cut up the Velveeta, it melts faster).

Topping

1 sleeve Ritz crackers

1 stick butter or margarine

Crush crackers. Melt butter over medium heat. Add crackers and mix well.

64809B-05

CHICKEN CASSEROLE

Diane Marsh

3 chicken breasts, cooked and chopped
1 lg. can cream of chicken soup
1 lg. can cream of mushroom soup
1 lg. container of sour cream
1 cup mayonnaise

$\frac{1}{2}$ cup chopped onion
1 bag broccoli, cooked according to directions
1 bag egg noodles, cooked
1 cup shredded cheese
1 box butter crackers, crushed

Combine soups, sour cream, mayo, onions, and broccoli; put aside. Cook noodles. Add noodles and chicken to soup mix. Put into a 9 x 13 pan. Combine crushed crackers and cheese, spread over casserole. Bake in 400° oven for about 45 minutes or until bubbly.

CHICKEN CRESCENT DINNER

Lynn Gibson
Original source: "A Taste of Hebron Cookbook"

1 (8-oz.) can crescent rolls
2 chicken breasts

1 can cream of chicken soup
1 can chicken broth

Makes 4 servings. Boil chicken breasts and cut into pieces. Spread chicken on rolls and roll up. Put in casserole dish. Mix cream of chicken soup with broth and pour over the rolled up chicken. Bake, uncovered at 350° for 30 minutes or until golden brown.

CHICKEN POT PIE

Vicky Brantley
Adapted from a recipe for easy cobbler

$1\frac{1}{2}$ cups chopped cooked chicken
1 chopped medium potato
$\frac{1}{2}$ chopped Vidalia onion
2 chopped carrots
1 sm. can of tiny green peas

2 chopped celery stalks
1 can cream of mushroom soup
$\frac{1}{2}$ cup melted margarine
$\frac{1}{2}$ cup buttermilk
$\frac{3}{4}$ cup self-rising flour
salt and pepper to taste

Makes 4 servings. Boil vegetables until tender and drain. Add salt and pepper. Add chicken and soup. Mix well. Add water if needed. Pour into casserole dish. Combine flour, melted margarine and buttermilk; mix well. Pour mixture over chicken and vegetable. Bake for 1 hour until crust is golden brown. An easy way to fix an old fashioned dish.

64809B-05

CHUCK WAGON CASSEROLE

Jane Miller, Winship Volunteer

½ cup onions, chopped
½ cup green bell pepper,
  chopped
1 lb. lean ground beef
1 can (15½ oz.) mild chili beans
  in sauce

¾ cup barbecue sauce
½ tsp. salt
1 pkg. (8½oz) corn muffin mix
1 (11-oz.) can Mexican-style
  corn, drained

Makes 6 servings. Preheat oven to 400°. Chop onion and bell pepper. Cook ground beef, onions and peppers in skillet until beef is no longer pink--medium heat for 8 to 10 minutes; drain. Stir in chili beans, BBQ sauce and salt. Bring to a boil. Spoon into 9-inch square baking dish or equivalent. Prepare corn muffin mix according to package directions, stir in corn. Spoon over meat mixture. Bake 30 minutes or until golden brown.

DINNER IN ONE CASSEROLE

Debbie Foster, Winship Volunteer

1 lb. lean ground beef
1 sm. onion, chopped
salt and pepper to taste
1 can French cut green beans,
  drained

1 can cheddar cheese soup
1 pkg. tater tots

Makes 4 servings. Layer in order in a rectangle casserole dish: raw hamburger, onion, salt and pepper, beans, soup mix, tater tots, and salt the top. Bake at 350° for 1 hour and let stand 10 minutes before serving.

Every part of my body works in beautiful synchronicity.

64809B-05

HAMBURGER PIE

Julie Whitehead, Winship Volunteer
Original source: Shirley Whitehead (Mom)

1 lb. hamburger
1 can condensed tomato soup
2 pie crusts
1½ cups chopped onion
1½ cups chopped celery
¼ tsp. salt (optional)

½ cup chopped green pepper
2 T. prepared mustard
¼ cup ketchup
½ cup sharp or extra sharp
   cheese, grated

Preheat oven to 425°. Cook on a stove top: hamburger, onions, celery and green pepper until vegetables are soft. Add soup, mustard, ketchup, cheese and salt. Put pie crust in a 9-inch deep dish pan. Pour in hamburger mixture and top with remaining crust. Score with fork. Bake for 35 to 40 minutes.

LAYERED CHICKEN ENCHILADA CASSEROLE

Andy Miller

1 T. vegetable oil
1 med. onion, chopped
2½ cups cooked shredded
   chicken breasts
1 (7-oz.) can diced green chilies
1 pkg. (1.25 oz.) taco seasoning
   mix

8 corn tortillas
1 (15-oz.) can kidney beans,
   drained
2 cups cheddar cheese
   shredded, divided
1 jar salsa

Makes 4 servings. Preheat oven to 350°. Grease 13 x 9 x 2 baking dish. Cook onion, stirring occasionally until tender. Remove from heat. Stir in chicken, chilies and seasoning mix. Layer half of tortillas in prepared baking dish. Top with chicken mixture, beans and 1 cup of cheese. Layer with remaining tortillas. Top with salsa and remaining cheese. Bake for 30 to 35 minutes or until heated through and cheese is melted. Can substitute red beans for kidney beans.

64809B-05

SMOKED SALMON BREAKFAST CASSEROLE

Mary Booth Thomas, Winship Volunteer

(8-oz.) smoked salmon cut into small pieces (bits and pieces will work)

2 cups broccoli, separated into small florets

2 bunches green onions, chopped

2 cups grated Swiss cheese

1 (8-oz.) pkg. cream cheese cut into small pieces

8 eggs

2 cups milk

1 cup Bisquick

salt and pepper to taste

Layer smoked salmon, broccoli, green onions and cheese in a casserole dish. Mix eggs, milk, baking mix, salt and pepper in a blender and blend until smooth. Pour into the casserole dish. Bake at 375° about 30 minutes or until it's firm.

Recipe Favorites

64809B-05

Sweets
& Desserts

Helpful Hints

- Egg whites need to be at room temperature for greater volume when whipped. Remember this when making meringue.

- When preparing several batches of pie dough, roll dough out between sheets of plastic wrap. Stack the discs in a pizza box, and keep the box in the freezer. Pull out the required crusts as needed.

- Place your pie plate on a cake stand when placing the pie dough in it and fluting the edges. The cake stand will make it easier to turn the pie plate, and you won't have to stoop over.

- Many kitchen utensils can be used to make decorative pie edges. For a scalloped edge, use a spoon. Crosshatched and herringbone patterns are achieved with a fork. For a sharply pointed effect, use a can opener to cut out points around the rim.

- Keep strawberries fresh for up to ten days by refrigerating them (unwashed) in an airtight container between layers of paper towels.

- When grating citrus peel, bits of peel are often stuck in the holes of the grater. Rather than waste the peel, you can easily brush it off by using a new, clean toothbrush.

- To core a pear, slice the pear in half lengthwise. Use a melon baller to cut out the central core, using a circular motion. Draw the melon baller to the top of the pear, removing the interior stem as you go.

- When cutting butter into flour for pastry dough, the process is easier if you cut the butter into small pieces before adding it to the flour.

- To keep the cake plate clean while frosting, slide 6-inch strips of waxed paper under each side of the cake. Once the cake is frosted and the frosting is set, pull the strips away leaving a clean plate.

- When decorating a cake with chocolate, you can make a quick decorating tube. Put chocolate in a heat-safe zipper-lock plastic bag. Immerse in simmering water until the chocolate is melted. Snip off the tip of one corner, and squeeze the chocolate out of the bag.

- Professionally decorated cakes have a silky, molten look. To get that appearance, frost your cake as usual, then use a hair dryer to blow-dry the surface until the frosting slightly melts.

- To ensure that you have equal amounts of batter in each pan when making a layered cake, use a kitchen scale to measure the weight.

SWEETS AND DESSERTS

ALMOND TORTE

Sue Gatliffre

1 (10 or 11-oz.) frozen Sara Lee
  pound cake (don't thaw)
2½ sticks unsalted butter, at
  room temperature
1½ cups powdered sugar
3 egg yolks

1 tsp. instant coffee
1 T. rum
1 tsp. vanilla
1 cup toasted almonds, finely
  chopped

Beat butter, until smooth, with an electric beater. Add sugar and beat. Beat in egg yolks, one at a time. Add a generous teaspoon of coffee which has been dissolved in a few drops of water. Add rum and vanilla; mix. Add ⅔ cup of almonds and mix. Cut cake into 5 layers. Frost each layer and frost top and sides of cake. Sprinkle cake top and sides with remaining almonds. Refrigerate. Remove from fridge at least an hour before serving. Serve at room temperature. Cake can be frozen.

ANGEL SUPREME

Judith Baker

Coconut instant pudding
(16-oz.) Cool Whip (or other
  non-dairy topping)
3 cups milk

(4-oz.) shredded coconut
(2-oz.) shredded almonds
1 Angel Food Cake

Makes 8 to 10 servings. Mix pudding according to package with milk. Cut Angel Food Cake in 1-inch squares. Layer ingredients in glass bowl, starting with cake, Cool Whip, then coconuts. End layers with Cool Whip and put almonds on top.

64809B-05

BANANA PUDDING

Annette Beck

15 lg. bananas (not quite ripe)
2 boxes Nabisco Vanilla Wafers
2 boxes French vanilla pudding

3 cups milk
2 lg. containers Cool Whip
1 can condensed milk

Mix vanilla pudding with 3 cups milk in large mixing bowl with good fitting top; shake until well mixed. Add 1 container of Cool Whip and condensed milk, mixing well. This is your pudding mix. Layer pudding mix, wafers and bananas until everything is used, ending with pudding, then top with the other container of Cool Whip. Be sure to use a very large mixing bowl or you can make two smaller puddings.

BLUEBERRY YUM YUM

Mary C. Dolvin

2 cups fresh (or frozen)
  blueberries
3 T. water
1 cup all-purpose flour
½ cup finely chopped pecans
½ cup margarine softened

1 (8-oz.) pkg. cream cheese
1 (8-oz.) container frozen
  whipped topping, thawed
1½ cups sugar, divided
¼ cup water
2 T. cornstarch

Makes 15 to 20 servings. Combine blueberries, 1 cup sugar and ¼ cup water in medium saucepan; cook over low heat until berries are soft (about 10 minutes). Combine cornstarch and 3 tablespoons water in a small bowl; add to boiling mixture. Bring to a boil over medium heat, stirring constantly; boil 1 minute. Set aside to cool. Combine flour, butter and pecans. Press evenly into a 13 x 9 x 2 baking dish. Bake at 350° for 20 minutes. Cool. Beat cream cheese and remaining ½ cup sugar at medium speed of electric mixer until smooth. Fold in whipped topping, spread evenly on crust. Spoon blueberry mixture over cream cheese topping; chill, cut into squares.

I am a blessing to every person with whom I come in contact.

64809B-05

CREAM CHEESE SQUARES

Nikki Elliott

2 8-count containers crescent
  rolls
2 (8-oz.) pkgs. cream cheese

¾ cup sugar
1 T. vanilla extract

Makes 12 servings. In a 9 x 13 pan, spread out one package of crescent rolls. Beat cream cheese, sugar and vanilla together. Spread on top of crescent rolls. Then spread second package of rolls on top. Brush on topping and sprinkle with cinnamon. Bake at 375° for about 20 minutes or until top is golden brown.

Topping

3 T. butter, melted

½ cup sugar

Mix together.

CUBAN FLAN

Susan Holton
Original Source: Rene Oglivie

4 eggs
1 can Coco Rallado
½ cup sugar
1 can sweetened condensed
  milk

1 tsp. vanilla
dash of salt

In a 1-quart casserole dish, burn sugar over low flame on top of stove. Coat bottom and half of sides with the browned sugar syrup; set aside. Separate eggs; beat yolks. Drain ⅓ liquid from can of coco rallado. Mix can of milk, beaten yolks, ¾ cup of water, salt, vanilla and coco. Beat egg whites to soft peak. Fold gently into first mixture. Pour into casserole. Bake in pan of boiling water, about 2-inches deep, or to level of the custard at 350° for 1½ to 2 hours. (I use a Pyrex casserole dish and bake with the top on.) Remove from water to cool. When at room temperature, put in refrigerator, chill overnight. After well chilled, remove by inverting over large plate. Let casserole stand for a while so that all the syrup will warm and drip onto the custard. Serve in wedges.

64809B-05

GRANDMA'S CREAMY RICE PUDDING

Sandra Murdock

3 cups cooked rice (great use
  for leftover rice)
3 cups milk
½ cup sugar

dash of salt
2 eggs, beaten
1 tsp. vanilla

Makes 8 servings. Combine rice, milk, sugar and salt. Cook over medium heat until thick and creamy (about 20 minutes). Remove from heat. Add a small amount of rice mixture to eggs; stir into remaining batter mixture. Cook 2 more minutes, stirring constantly. Add butter and vanilla. Spoon into buttered 1½-quart dish. Serve warm or cold.

HEAVENLY HASH

Florence Greeson

5 bananas
5 slices pineapple
30 marshmallows
3 egg whites
1 med. bottle cherries

3 cups heavy cream, whipped
¾ to 1 cup sugar
1 tsp. vanilla
1½ cups pecans, chopped

Cut fruits and marshmallows into small pieces. Beat egg whites until stiff; add whipped cream. Add sugar and vanilla. Fold in fruits, marsh-mallows and nuts. Place mixture in a large bowl. Cover and refrigerate for at least 3 hours before serving.

MOM'S FUDGE

Claire Smith

3 (6-oz.) pkgs. chocolate chips
2 sticks margarine
1 lg. can Carnation evaporated
  milk

5 cups sugar
1½ tsp. vanilla flavoring
1 cup pecans, chopped, optional

Add milk and sugar in a large pot on medium heat. Bring to a boil. Boil for 7 minutes. In a separate bowl, add chocolate chips, vanilla and margarine. Pour milk and sugar mixture over chocolate chip mixture. Beat until chips are melted. Pour mixture into buttered pans. Leave out on counter until cooled, then refrigerate.

64809B-05

PEACH FLOATING ISLAND

Vicki Devlin

Custard

⅓ cup flour	1 T. unsalted butter
½ cup sugar	1 tsp. vanilla extract
2 cups milk	diced peaches (fresh or canned)
2 eggs	

Makes 6 servings. Sift flour, ½ cup sugar and salt into top of double boiler. Whisk in ½ cup milk to make a paste and add remaining milk gradually. Beat in eggs. Put pan over simmering water and cook, stirring for 15 to 20 minutes or until smooth and thick. Remove from heat; add butter, vanilla and diced peaches. Let cool.

Meringue

3 egg whites (at room temperature)	¼ tsp. cream of tartar
	½ cup sugar

Beat egg whites until frothy. Add cream of tartar and beat until soft peaks hold. Add ½ cup sugar, 2 tablespoons at a time until stiff and glossy. Heat broiler 5 minutes. Spoon meringue onto ¼-inch of boiling water in shallow pan. Broil until toasted (or bake in oven). Lift out with slotted spoon, draining off water and place on top of custard covering peaches.

POOR MAN'S CUPCAKE

Susan Ottinger

1 cup Crisco	½ tsp. salt
2 cups sugar	½ tsp. cloves
3 cups hot water	1½ tsp. nutmeg
1 pkg. raisins	1½ tsp. cinnamon
4 to 5 cups flour	1 tsp. vanilla
1 T. baking soda	

Makes 3 dozen cupcakes. Preheat oven to 350°. Boil first 4 ingredients for 10 minutes and set aside until cool. When cool, add flour, baking soda and spices; stir. Fill cupcake papers ½ full and bake at 350° for 25 minutes.

64809B-05

PUMPKIN SQUARES

Barbara Faro

4 eggs
1 cup Wesson or vegetable oil
2 cups flour
2 tsp. baking soda
1 tsp. salt

1²/₃ cups sugar
1 (16-oz.) can pumpkin
2 tsp. baking powder
2 tsp. cinnamon

Makes 12 servings. Beat together eggs, oil, sugar and pumpkin. Add salt, soda and baking powder to flour. Blend all together and add cinnamon. Bake at 350° for 25 to 30 minutes in a 10 x 15 x 1 ungreased pan. Frosting: 3-oz. cream cheese, ³/₄ cup butter, 1 tsp. vanilla and 2 cups confectioners sugar. Mix and frost cake. Sprinkle with chopped walnuts.

RICE KRISPIES SCOTCHAROOS

Laurel Fye

1 cup sugar
1 cup Karo light syrup
1 cup peanut butter (smooth, not crunchy)

6 cups Rice Krispies (or the generic equivalent)
(6-oz.) pkg. chocolate chips
(6-oz.) pkg. butterscotch chips

Combine sugar and Karo. Bring to a boil, stirring constantly (not a full rolling boil, just a few bubbles). Remove from heat. Stir in peanut butter and Rice Krispies into a 9 x 13 pan. Work quickly! Let it cool. Melt chips and spread over bars. Use a sharp knife to cut through bars once chocolate/butterscotch mixture has set.

STRAWBERRY SUPREME MOLD

Elaine Koenig

1 lg. pkg. strawberry gelatin
1 can pink lemonade
1 pt. vanilla ice cream
1 qt. fresh strawberries

2 cups water
2 (10-oz.) pkgs. frozen strawberries, drained
¹/₂ cup pecans, chopped

Makes 8 to 10 servings. Follow the directions on the gelatin package, using only 2 cups water. Add melted ice cream and melted lemonade. Add juice from one package of drained strawberries. Add 2 packages of drained strawberries, then add pecans. Refrigerate mixture in a ring mold until firm. When serving, fill center of ring mold with fresh strawberries.

64809B-05

CAKES

APPLESAUCE CAKE
(Diabetic Recipe)

Tiffany Barrett
Original source: Splenda

1 cup all-purpose flour
1 tsp. baking powder
½ tsp. baking soda
2 tsp. cinnamon
½ tsp. ginger
½ cup margarine

½ cup molasses
½ cup egg substitute
1 tsp. vanilla extract
1 cup Splenda Grandular
½ cup applesauce

Preheat oven to 350°. Spray a square pan with cooking spray. Stir flour, baking soda, baking powder, cinnamon and ginger. In a large bowl, beat margarine and molasses with an electric mixer for 1 minute. Add egg substitute and vanilla; blend for 1 minute. Add Splenda and beat until smooth. Add flour mixture and applesauce beat on low speed until mixed. Spread batter into pan and bake for 30 minutes.

BLACK FOREST DUMP CAKE

Jane Miller, Winship Volunteer

1 (8-oz.) can crushed pineapple
1 (21-oz.) can cherry pie filling
1 (18.5-oz.) pkg. devil's food
 cake mix

1 cup chopped pecans
½ cup butter or margarine,
 melted
whipped topping

Makes 15 servings. Drain pineapple, reserving the liquid. Spread pineapple in a lightly greased 13 x 9 x 2 pan. Add pie filling, spreading gently. Sprinkle dry cake mix on pie filling, top with pecans. Combine butter and reserved pineapple liquid; drizzle on mixture in pan. Bake at 350° for 35 to 40 minutes. Cut into squares, top with whipped topping.

64809B-05

CAKE WITH PEANUT BUTTER FROSTING

Lynn Gibson

1 box Jiffy yellow cake mix
  (small 1 layer)
¼ cup peanut butter

¼ cup milk
1 cup light brown sugar

Makes 6 servings. Prepare cake according to directions on cake mix box in a 8 or 9-inch square pan. Combine peanut butter, milk and brown sugar on warm cake.

A peaceful confidence flows through my being.

108

CHOCOLATE CHEESECAKE

Margaret (Mugsy) Schwab

Crust

1¼ cups graham cracker crumbs (9 crackers)

2 T. sugar (2-oz.) melted butter

Line outside of springform pan with heavy aluminum foil, shiny side out. Put circle of parchment paper on bottom of pan so cake can be transferred to a serving plate. Butter inside of pan. Mix graham cracker crumbs with sugar, add melted butter and press into pan evenly. Refrigerate.

Filling

(9-oz.) bittersweet baking chocolate
(6-oz.) rum (dark rum for flavor)
1 lb. cream cheese

¾ cup extra fine sugar
½ cup sour cream
1 T. vanilla extract
5 lg. eggs

Melt chocolate with rum over low heat (1 minute); set aside. (Easiest and safest way to melt the chocolate is to use a double boiler. I sort of measure and throw chocolate into the pan with very hot water below it and let it start to melt as I measure things out) With an electric mixer, beat cream cheese until fluffy. Gradually beat in extra fine sugar, sour cream and vanilla extract. Add eggs, one at a time; mix well. Place bowl over hot water and stir until completely smooth, do not over mix. Pour 10 ounces of batter into another bowl and set aside. Mix remaining batter with chocolate using a whisk, then stir until smooth over hot water. Take springform pan from refrigerator and gently fill with chocolate batter. Gently pour plain batter over the top and make swirls in the batter with a fork. Set the pan on a large piece of heavy aluminum foil and fold up the sides. Carefully set pan in larger roasting pan. Pour boiling water into roasting pan until it is halfway up the sides of the cheesecake pan. Cook at 325° for 45 minutes. Be careful not to over-cook. The cheesecake should still jiggle and will firm up after chilling. Loosen from the sides of the pan by running a thin metal spatula around the inside rim. Let cool for 30 minutes, then chill in refrigerator, loosely covered for at least 4 hours. Unmold and transfer to a cake plate.

64809B-05

CHOCOLATE CHIP CAKE

Debbie Foster, Winship Volunteer
Original source: Sarah Tauber

1 Duncan Hines Devil's Food
Cake Mix
1 sm. instant chocolate pudding
mix

(12-oz.) chocolate chips
1¾ cups milk
2 eggs

Stir all and add chips. Pour into bundt pan sprayed with cooking spray.
Bake at 350° for 50 to 55 minutes. Serve hot or warm. Fantastic for
quick desserts; tastes best warm.

CHOCOLATE-AMARETTO LAYER CAKE

Susan Holton
Original Source: Sandra Moss

1 pkg. devil's food cake mix
1⅓ cups water
3 lg. eggs
½ cup vegetable oil
12 T. amaretto liqueur
¾ tsp. almond extract
3 cups semi-sweet chocolate
chips (about 18-oz.)

¼ cup (½ stick) unsalted butter
¼ cup whipping cream
⅔ cup sour cream
1 cup powdered sugar
1 cup slivered almonds, toasted

Preheat oven to 350°. Grease three 9-inch diameter cake pans. Combine cake mix, 1⅓ cups water, eggs, oil, 3 tablespoons amaretto and
½ teaspoon almond extract in large bowl; whisk until well blended. Mix
in 1 cup chocolate chips. Divide batter among prepared pans. Bake
cakes until tester inserted into center comes out clean. Cool cakes in
pans for 10 minutes. Run knife around pan sides. Turn cakes out onto
racks; cool completely. Brush each cake layer with 2 tablespoons amaretto. Combine butter and cream in medium saucepan. Stir over medium-
low heat until butter melts and mixture comes to simmer. Remove from
heat. Add remaining 2 cups chocolate chips and whisk until melted. Mix
in remaining 3 tablespoons amaretto. Cool until barely lukewarm, about
5 minutes. Whisk in sour cream and remaining ¼ teaspoon almond
extract, then powdered sugar. Refrigerate frosting just until thick enough
to spread, whisking occasionally, about 10 minutes. Place 1 cake layer
on platter and spread ⅓ cup frosting over top. Top with second cake
layer. Spread ⅓ cup frosting over top. Top with third cake layer. Spread
remaining frosting over top and sides of cake. Press nuts around bottom
2-inches of cake. Chill 2 hours. Cover with cake dome; keep chilled.
This recipe can be made 2 days prior to serving.

64809B-05

CREAM CHEESE POUND CAKE

Franklin L. Geer

3 sticks oleo
1 (8-oz.) pkg. cream cheese
3 cups sugar

6 eggs
3 cups plain flour
1 tsp. vanilla

Cream butter, sugar, cheese and vanilla. Add 2 eggs and 1 cup of flour. Beat well. Add 2 more eggs and 1 cup of flour. Beat well and scrape from bottom with spatula to make sure batter is well mixed. Add remaining 2 eggs and 1 cup of flour. Beat well, dough will be stiff. Start in cold oven and ungreased tube pan. Turn oven to 300° and bake for 1 hour and 45 minutes (some ovens may take 5 to 10 minutes longer).

DATE NUT CAKE
(A diabetic cake)

Georgia Miller

½ cup butter or margarine
2 eggs
1 T. liquid sweetener
2 cups flour
1½ tsp. soda
¼ tsp. cloves
½ tsp. cinnamon

1 cup plain dates, chopped
1 tsp. vanilla
1½ cups applesauce,
   unsweetened
1 cup chopped pecans or
   walnuts

Blend eggs, butter, sweetener and vanilla. Sift together flour, soda and spices. Add to first mixture. Fold in dates, applesauce and nuts. Bake in a 9 x 9 pan at 350° for 25 minutes or until done.

I love waking up in the morning to greet a bright new day.

64809B-05

FUDGEY PECAN CAKE

Dorothy Ford

¾ cup butter, melted
1½ cups sugar
1½ tsp. vanilla extract
3 egg yolks
½ cup plus 1 T. cocoa
½ cup flour

3 T. oil
3 T. water
¾ cup finely chopped pecans
3 egg whites, room temperature
⅛ tsp. cream of tartar
⅛ tsp. salt

Makes 12 servings. Line bottom of 9-inch springform pan with foil; butter foil and sides of pan. Set aside. Combine melted butter, sugar and vanilla in a large bowl; beat well. Add egg yolks, one at a time, beating well after each. Blend in cocoa, flour, oil and water. Beat well. Stir in pecans. Beat egg whites, cream of tartar and salt in a small bowl until stiff. Carefully fold into chocolate mixture. Pour into pan. Bake at 350° for 45 minutes, or until top begins to crack slightly (cake will not taste done in the center). Cool for 1 hour. Cover and chill until firm. Remove sides of pan and pour glaze over cake. Allow to run down sides. Spread glaze evenly on top and let harden. Garnish with pecan halves. Glaze: Melt chocolate chips and whipping cream--do not boil. Remove from heat. Cool, stir occasionally until mixture begins to thicken, about 10 to 15 minutes.

JEWISH APPLE CAKE

Judy Bennett

3 cups flour
4 eggs
1 tsp. baking powder
2 cups sugar
1 cup oil

⅓ cup orange juice
2½ tsp. vanilla
3 apples sliced thin (remove
  skin)
1 tsp. cinnamon

Makes 10 to 12 servings, depending on the size of the slices. Sift flour, baking powder and 1½ cups sugar together into a large bowl. Save ½ cup sugar. Make indentation in the center and add orange juice, vanilla, eggs and oil. Mix until smooth. Grease and flour a 9 or 10-inch tube pan. Put a layer of batter, then a layer of apples, alternating three times; ending with apples on top. Using ½ cup sugar add 1 tsp. cinnamon and sprinkle on top of apples between layers and on top of cake. Bake 1 hour and 14 minutes at 350°.

64809B-05

KEY LIME CAKE

Maureen Moran

1 box Lemon Supreme cake mix
1 (3-oz.) box lime Jello
1½ cups vegetable oil

5 eggs
½ cup orange juice

Mix above ingredients together. Beat 2 to 3 minutes at medium speed. Pour into 3 round greased pans. Bake at 350° for 25 minutes.

Glaze

4 T. confectioners sugar   ½ cup key lime juice

Mix confectioners sugar and lime juice together. While layers are still warm, pierce with toothpick and drizzle over all three layers.

Icing

1 box confectioners sugar
1 (8-oz.) pkg. softened cream
  cheese

1 stick butter

Cream butter and cheese together, blend in confectioners sugar. Ice cake when cooled.

64809B-05

LAYERS OF DELIGHT

Lynn Gibson

First Layer

1 (19-oz.) pkg. Pillsbury Brownie Classics Brownie Mix Traditional Fudge	½ cup canola oil ¼ cup water 3 lg. eggs

Second Layer

3 (8-oz.) pkgs. cream cheese, softened	2 lg. eggs 1⅓ cups powdered sugar

Makes 12 servings. Heat oven to 325°. Grease bottom and sides of 9 x 13 pan. Prepare brownie mix according to package directions for cake-like brownies. Spread batter in prepared pan. In a small bowl, combine cream cheese and 3 eggs. Beat until well combined at low speed. Gradually add powdered sugar while beating at low speed. Spoon cream cheese mixture so that it completely covers the top of the brownie batter layer. Cover pan with aluminum foil and bake for approximately 1 hour and 15 minutes or until center is almost set. Cool completely. Spread top of dessert with frosting. Refrigerate for at least 4 hours or overnight prior to serving. Store in refrigerator.

Third Layer

1 (16-oz.) can Pillsbury Creamy Supreme Frosting Chocolate Fudge Flavor

Today, I discover my new strengths.

64809B-05

LEMONADE CAKE

Stella Kazazian, Winship Volunteer

1 (3-oz.) pkg. lemon gelatin
¾ cup boiling water
1½ cups sugar
¾ cup vegetable oil
4 eggs
2½ cups all-purpose flour
2½ tsp. baking powder

1 tsp. salt
2 T. lemon juice
1 T. grated lemon peel
1 T. lemon extract
1 (6-oz.) can frozen lemonade
½ cup powdered sugar

Preheat oven to 350°. Dissolve gelatin in boiling water and set aside to cool. Mix together sugar and oil. Add eggs, one at a time, beating well after each addition. In separate bowl mix together flour, baking powder and salt. Add flour mixture alternately with gelatin mixture to egg mixture, beginning and ending with dry ingredients. Beat well after each addition. Stir in lemon juice, peel and lemon extract. Pour batter into greased and floured 10-inch tube pan or bundt pan and bake for 1 hour without opening door. While cake is baking, thaw lemonade and stir in powdered sugar. Beat until smooth. Punch holes in top of cake and pour lemonade mixture over cake while still warm. Let cool in pan before removing.

MILLION DOLLAR POUND CAKE

Kay Adams

1 lb. (4 sticks) butter at room
  temperature
3 cups granulated sugar
6 eggs (at room temperature)
4 cups all-purpose flour, sifted 4
  times

¾ cup milk (at room
  temperature)
1 tsp. lemon extract (or almond
  extract)
1 tsp. vanilla extract

Makes 16 servings. Preheat oven to 300°. Have butter, eggs and milk at room temperature (this really does make a difference). Combine sugar, 1 cup at a time, with the butter and beat until light and fluffy. Add the eggs, one at a time, beating well after each addition. Add the flour to the creamed mixture, ½ cup at a time, beating well after each addition. Stir in milk and extracts. Pour batter into a well-greased and floured 10-inch tube pan. Bake 1½ to 2 hours, until cake is done. Remarks: "The Staff of Life," according to my father-in-law, John Adams, who is now a patient at Winship.

64809B-05

ORANGE CARROT CAKE

Claire Smith

1¼ cup vegetable oil
1 cup light brown sugar, packed
1 cup granulated sugar
4 lg. eggs
2 cups plain flour
1 tsp. baking powder

1 tsp. baking soda
1 tsp. salt
1 tsp. cinnamon
3 cups carrots, shredded
grated zest of 1 orange
1 tsp. orange extract

Beat together oil, brown sugar, granulated sugar, and add eggs. Whisk together flour, baking powder, baking soda, salt and cinnamon. Add dry ingredients to sugar mixture. Stir in carrots, zest and extract. Pour batter into a 9 x 12 pan that has been greased and floured. Bake at 325° for 35 to 40 minutes or until done.

Creamy Orange Frosting

(12-oz.) cream cheese, softened
¾ cup butter or margarine,
  softened

6 cups confectioner's sugar
1 tsp. orange extract
finely grated zest of 1 orange

Beat cream cheese, butter and zest until smooth. Add sugar, beating until smooth. Blend in extract. Ice cooled cake.

ORANGE SLICE CAKE

Julie Whitehead, Winship Volunteer

1 cup butter
4 eggs
½ cup buttermilk
1 pkg. frozen coconut
1 lb. candy orange slices,
  chopped

2 cups sugar
3½ cups all-purpose flour
1 tsp. soda
1 cup chopped pecans
1 lb. dates, chopped

Glaze

2 cups confectioners sugar

1 cup orange juice

Preheat oven to 250°. Cream butter and sugar. Add eggs one at a time to butter and sugar mixture. Add flour (reserve ½ cup), soda and buttermilk alternately. Roll nuts, candy and dates in ½ cup flour and add to batter. Bake in a tube pan 2½ to 3 hours. When cake is ready to come from the oven, prepare glaze. Pour over cake while hot. Leave in the pan overnight. This cake cooks heavy, almost like a fruit cake.

64809B-05

PINA COLADA CHEESECAKE

Lucy Finney

1¾ cups graham cracker
  crumbs
¾ cup chopped pecans, toasted
1 T. sugar
6 T. unsalted butter, melted
3 (8-oz.) pkgs. cream cheese
½ cup sugar
5 eggs

1 (8-oz.) can crushed pineapple,
  drained (reserve juice)
1 cup sour cream
1 cup cream of coconut (Goya
  or Coco Lopez)
⅓ cup rum (Bacardi)
4 tsp. pineapple juice

Stir together first 4 ingredients; press into bottom and 1-inch up on sides of springform pan lined with parchment paper. Beat cream cheese and sugar at medium speed with electric mixer until fluffy. Add eggs, one at a time, beating well after each addition. Add pineapple and next 4 ingredients, beating until blended. Pour into crust. Bake at 325° for 1 hour and 15 minutes, or until center is almost set. Cool on wire rack. Spread glaze over top. Chill at least 8 hours. Garnish with whipped cream and toasted coconut.

Glaze

1 T. cornstarch
1 T. water
1 (8-oz.) can crushed pineapple

¼ cup sugar
2 T. lemon juice

Stir together cornstarch and water until smooth. Mix with the rest of the ingredients in a saucepan and cook over medium heat, stirring occasionally until thickened and bubbly. Remove from heat and let cool completely before spreading over cheesecake.

64809B-05

PUMPKIN SPICE CHEESECAKE

Susan Holton
Original Source: Jenny Puchferran

Crust

2 cups gingersnap crumbs
¼ cup sugar

4 T. melted margarine or butter

Makes 12 or more servings. Grind gingersnaps to crumbs in a food processor or use a rolling pin on cookies encased in a heavy-duty plastic bag. Combine crumbs, sugar and melted margarine and mix until blended. Press onto bottom of a 9-inch springform pan. Wrap the bottom of pan in heavy-duty foil to prevent butter leaks. Set aside.

Filling

3 (8-oz.) pkgs. reduced fat
  cream cheese, softened
1 (14-oz.) can sweetened
  condensed milk
2 cups pumpkin purée (1-15 oz.
  can)
3 lg. eggs

1½ tsp. ground cinnamon
1½ tsp. ground ginger
½ tsp. freshly grated nutmeg
pinch of salt
1 tsp. pure vanilla extract
1 tsp. almond extract

Combine cream cheese and condensed milk in a large bowl and beat with an electric mixer at high speed for 2 minutes. Add pumpkin, eggs, spices, vanilla and almond extracts and beat for 1 minute. Pour over prepared crust. Bake at 375° for 65 to 70 minutes, or until set. Cool completely on a rack. Refrigerate at least 2 hours. May be made several days ahead.

Topping

1½ cups sour cream
¼ cup sugar

1 tsp. vanilla

Mix the above ingredients and pour over the cheesecake when first removed from the oven. Put back in the oven for approximately 5 minutes. Then remove from the oven and sprinkle with chopped nuts and set on rack to cool. To serve: Loosen cake from sides of springform pan and remove form. Slice in narrow wedges and serve. (The recipe does not call for a topping, but I like to add the above ingredients).

I hold myself and others with loving thoughts.

64809B-05

RUM CAKE

Marion Waaland
Original source: Baccardi Rum

½ cup chopped pecans
1 (18-oz.) pkg. yellow cake mix
  with pudding in mix
½ cup dark rum

½ cup water
½ cup salad oil
3 eggs

Makes 12 servings. Grease and flour 10-inch tube pan or bundt pan. Sprinkle chopped pecans over bottom of the pan. Combine cake mix, rum, water, salad oil and eggs. Beat exactly 2 minutes at medium speed of electric mixer. Pour batter in pan. Bake at 325° for 1 hour. Allow cake to cool for 10 minutes; invert on rack. Poke holes all over and brush with glaze--use all of the glaze. Wrap tightly in plastic wrap and aluminum foil. Freezes well.

Glaze

1 cup sugar
½ cup butter or margarine

¼ cup water
¼ cup dark rum

Combine all ingredients and boil 2 to 3 minutes.

PIES

CHERRY-BERRY PEACH PIE

Judy Bennett

3 cups sliced peeled peaches
  (about 6)
1 cup fresh blueberries
1 cup pitted halved fresh sweet
  cherries
1 T. fresh lemon juice
¼ cup packed light brown
  sugar

½ cup granulated sugar
3 T. flour
⅛ tsp. salt
¼ tsp. cinnamon
pastry for 2-crust 9 inch pie
milk
granulated sugar

Makes 6 to 8 servings. Mix together peaches, blueberries and cherries in a large bowl. Sprinkle with lemon juice. Gently stir in brown sugar, granulated sugar, flour, salt and cinnamon. Line a 9-inch pie plate with half of pastry. Trim overhang to 1-inch. Turn fruit into pie. Cover pie with remaining pastry. Fold edges under and seal edges. Brush with milk and sprinkle with sugar. Bake at 450° for 10 minutes. Reduce to 350° and bake 45 to 50 minutes until pastry is brown and fruit is tender. Refrigerate pie after cooled. Even better the next day.

64809B-05

COOKIE PIE

Denene Johnson

1 bag chocolate chip cookies
1 tub of Cool Whip

1 cup milk
1 bag coconut flakes

Crush about 10 cookies and spread on the bottom of round, ungreased pie pan--this will keep the pie from sticking to the bottom of the pan. Dip cookies into milk until soft but not mushy and place on top of crushed cookies. Spread some Cool Whip on top as to seal from edge to edge. Sprinkle coconut flakes. Repeat layers once or twice ending with whipped topping and flakes. Cover pie with wax paper and place in freezer for 45 minutes. Slice like a pie and enjoy!

GERMAN CHOCOLATE PIE

Penelope Estes

½ cup butter
½ (4-oz.) bar of Baker's Sweet
  German Chocolate (green
  package)
3 eggs

1 cup sugar
½ cup all-purpose flour
½ cup chopped pecans
½ tsp. vanilla
½ cup coconut if desired

Melt butter and chocolate in the microwave. Beat eggs, add sugar and flour; mix well. Combine with melted mixture; add pecans, vanilla and coconut if desired. Pour into greased 9-inch pie pan. Bake at 325° for 45 minutes. Serve with whip cream. "I always double this recipe. Makes more sense to use all the chocolate, and you have two pies for the work of one!!! This is not an attractive pie, but it does taste good."

LEMON PIE

Georgia Miller

1 pkg. instant sugar-free vanilla
  pudding
2 cups milk

½ of 8-oz. Cool Whip
1 pkg. sugar free lemonade mix
Graham cracker crust

Combine pudding and milk and beat until thickened. Mix in ½ of 8-oz. Cool Whip. Stir in 1 package sugar-free lemonade mix. Pour in a Graham cracker crust. Put in refrigerator.

64809B-05

SWEET POTATO PIE

Mary Hutchins

2½ lbs. sweet potatoes
½ tsp. nutmeg
1 tsp. vanilla
¼ cup melted butter
¼ cup evaporated milk

½ cup sugar
½ tsp. cinnamon
1 tsp. lemon flavoring
2 eggs beaten
2 9 inch pie unbaked pie crusts

2 pies feed 16 people. Boil sweet potatoes in skins until tender--use the dark, red-skinned sweet potatoes or yams. Drain, peel and mash well. Blend in sugar, nutmeg, cinnamon, vanilla, lemon and butter. Fold in eggs. Add evaporated milk and beat mixture until fluffy, using an electric mixer. Pour in pie shells and bake in 300° over 35 to 40 minutes or until lightly browned.

COOKIES

CHOCOLATE CHIP COOKIES

Mary Leigh Harper

2¼ cups all-purpose flour
1 T. baking soda
1 tsp. salt
1 cup (2 sticks) butter, softened
¾ cup granulated sugar

¾ cup packed brown sugar
1 tsp. vanilla extract
2 eggs
2 cups (12-oz. pkg) semi-sweet
   chocolate morsels

Makes 12 servings. Combine flour, baking soda and salt in a small bowl. Beat butter, sugar, brown sugar and vanilla in a large bowl. Add eggs one at a time, beating well after each addition. Gradually beat in flour mixture. Stir in morsels. Drop by rounded tablespoonfuls on ungreased baking sheet. Bake 8 to 10 minutes or until golden brown at 350°. From scratch--"the best ever!!"

64809B-05

CHOCOLATE CHIP PUDDING COOKIES

Susan M. Witek

2¼ cups unsifted all-purpose
  flour
1 tsp. baking soda
1 cup butter or margarine,
  softened
¼ cup granulated sugar
¾ cup firmly packed brown
  sugar

1 (12-oz.) pkg. chocolate chips
1 (4-oz.) pkg. instant pudding &
  pie mixture (chocolate)*
1 tsp. vanilla
2 eggs
1 cup chopped nuts (optional)

Mix flour with baking soda. Combine butter, sugar, pudding mix and vanilla in a large bowl. Beat until smooth and creamy. Beat in egg; gradually add flour mixture, then stir in chips and nuts (batter will be stiff). Drop by rounded teaspoon onto ungreased baking sheet, about 2-inches apart. Bake at 375° for 8 to 10 minutes. *Or use butter pecan, butterscotch, French vanilla or vanilla pudding mix.

Today, I let my excitement for life's possibilities spur me on to greater things.

64809B-05

CHOCOLATE COVERED OREO BALLS

Laurel Fye

1 (16-oz.) pkg. Oreos*
1 (8-oz.) pkg. cream cheese,
  softened

chocolate disks for candy
  making**

Using a food processor or electric food chopper, crush the Oreo cookies (as many as the equipment can handle at a time) until they are very fine in consistency and all cookies have been crushed. Transfer to a large mixing bowl. Add the softened cream cheese to the crumb mixture. Mix thoroughly using a stand mixer or a strong hand mixer. Dough will be sticky--DO NOT add more cookies. Roll dough into small balls (maybe as round as a quarter or as big as a Jacks ball) and place in rows on a cookie sheet. Once the sheet is full, place in the freezer for 5 to 7 minutes or in the fridge for 8 to 10 minutes--just long enough for the cookie balls to get cold. Do not freeze. While the cookie balls are chilling, melt the chocolate disks according to the package directions. Be careful not to burn the chocolate. Once the balls are cold, dip them one at a time into the melted chocolate and then return them to the cookie sheet. Once the sheet is filled with chocolate covered Oreo balls, return to the fridge so the chocolate can set. This should take about 10 minutes. After the chocolate is set, place the cookie balls in an airtight container and store in the fridge. ENJOY!!! *DO NOT use Double Stuff--use only Oreos. However, you can experiment by trying the flavored Oreos (mint, peanut butter, etc.). **Any color/flavor of the chocolate disks should work. You can customize them for the holidays using red/green or for bridal showers by dipping them in chocolate the colors of the wedding.

CRISP SUGAR COOKIES

Elizabeth Evans

½ cup butter (no substitutes)
¾ cup sugar
1 egg
1½ tsp. vanilla

1½ cups flour
1 tsp. baking powder
¼ tsp. salt

Cream butter, sugar, egg and vanilla. Combine dry ingredients and blend into wet ingredients. Chill dough 4 hours or more. Roll out, invite the kids and cut into cute shapes. Bake 10 to 12 minutes on 350°.

64809B-05

GINGER MOLASSES COOKIES

Debbie Foster, Winship Volunteer

Beat:

1 cup Crisco
½ cup Crisco oil

2 cups sugar

Add:

2 eggs
½ cup molasses
4 tsp. baking soda
1 tsp. ground cloves
2 tsp. ground ginger

1 tsp. salt
About 4 cups or more flour
(enough to make a medium
dough--not sticky or hard)

Makes about 4 to 5 dozen. Bake at 375°. Roll into balls; roll in sugar. Bake on a greased sheet for about 10 minutes.

LEMON SQUARES

Sarah Burt
Original source: Cooking Light

Crust

¼ cup granulated sugar
3 T. butter or stick margarine,
  softened

1 cup all-purpose flour

Preheat oven 350°. To prepare the crust, beat ¼ cup granulated sugar and the butter at medium speed of a mixer until creamy. Lightly spoon 1 cup of flour into a dry measuring cup; level with a knife. Gradually add 1 cup of flour to sugar mixture, beating at low speed until mixture resembles fine crumbs. Gently press mixture into bottom of an 8-inch square baking pan. Bake at 350° for 15 minutes; cool on a rack.

Topping

3 lg. eggs
¾ cup granulated sugar
2 tsp. grated lemon rind
⅓ cup fresh lemon juice

3 T. all-purpose flour
½ tsp. baking powder
⅛ tsp. salt
2 tsp. powdered sugar

Beat eggs at medium speed until foamy. Add ¾ cup granulated sugar and next 5 ingredients (¾ cup granulated sugar through salt), and beat until well-blended. Pour mixture over partially baked crust. Bake at 350° for 20 to 25 minutes or until set. Cool on wire rack. Sift powdered sugar evenly over top.

64809B-05

NANA QUEHL'S MOLASSES COOKIES

Kathy Fonder

¾ cup shortening	1 tsp. ginger
1 cup white sugar	1 tsp. cloves
4 T. molasses	½ tsp. salt
2 sm. tsp. baking soda	2 cups flour
1 tsp. cinnamon	

Dissolve baking soda, cinnamon, ginger and cloves in molasses. Cream shortening and sugar; add remaining ingredients. Form dough into small balls and flatten with a glass (dust the bottom with sugar). Bake at 350° for 10 minutes. Wait 1 to 2 minutes before removing cookies off cookie sheet.

OREO DESSERT

First Layer

1 (16-oz.) pkg. Oreo cookies	2 sm. containers Cool Whip
1 stick butter	2 sm. packages instant
1 (8-oz.) pkg. cream cheese	chocolate pudding
1 cup powdered sugar	3 cups milk

Crush Oreo cookies and set ¼ cup aside. Melt butter and mix with cookies. Press into 9 x 13 pan and put in freezer for 5 minutes. Mix powdered sugar and room temperature cream cheese. Fold in container of Cool Whip. Spread over cookie base.

Second Layer

Mix chocolate pudding mix and milk until thickened. (Ignore pudding package instructions). Spread over first layer.

Third Layer

Spread second container of Cool Whip on top. Sprinkle with remaining cookie crumbs.

64809B-05

SPICE COOKIES

Judy Baker
Interpreted from "Good Housekeeping: A Very Merry
Christmas Cookbook 2003"

5½ cups all-purpose flour	1 cup butter or margarine (2
1 tsp. ground cinnamon	sticks), softened
1 tsp. ground allspice	1¼ cups packed light brown
½ tsp. ground nutmeg	sugar
½ tsp. baking soda	1 (12-oz.) jar dark molasses
½ tsp. salt	Ornamental Frosting, optional

Makes about 4 dozen cookies. In a large bowl combine flour, cinnamon, allspice, nutmeg, baking soda and salt. In another large bowl, with mixer at low speed, beat butter with brown sugar until blended. Increase speed to high; beat until light and creamy. At low speed, beat molasses until blended, then beat in 3 cups flour mixture. With spoon, stir in remaining flour mixture. Divide dough into 4 equal pieces. Wrap each piece in plastic wrap and freeze at least 1 hour or refrigerate overnight, until dough is firm enough to roll. Preheat oven to 350°. On well-floured surface, with floured rolling pin, roll out 1 piece of dough ⅛-inch thick, keeping remaining dough refrigerated (dough will be soft). With floured 3 to 4-inch assorted cookie cutters, cut dough into as many cookies as possible; reserve trimmings. Place cookies, about 1-inch apart, on ungreased large cookie sheet. Bake cookies 8 to 10 minutes, just until browned. Cool cookies on cookie sheet 5 minutes. With wide spatula, transfer cookies to wire rack to cool completely. Repeat with remaining dough and trimmings. Optional: When cookies are cool, prepare Ornamental Frosting--use to decorate cookies as desired. Set cookies aside to allow frosting to dry completely, about 1 hour.

Ornamental Frosting

Makes about 3 cups. In bowl, with mixer at medium speed, beat 1 package (16-oz.) confectioners' sugar, 3 tablespoons meringue powder and ⅓ cup warm water about 5 minutes, until blended and mixture is so stiff that a knife drawn through it leaves a clean-cut path. If you like, tint frosting with food colorings or food-color pastes--keep covered with plastic wrap to prevent drying out. With small metal spatula, artist's paintbrushes or decorating bags with small writing tips, decorate cookies with frosting. (You may need to thin frosting with a little warm water.)

I move through all situations with poise and confidence.

64809B-05

BARS & BROWNIES

CHOCOLATE NUT WAFERS

Chosh Waldo Dacey
Original source: "My step-grandmother's Canadian
mother's recipe"

2 squares semi-sweet chocolate
or cocoa equivalent
½ cup margarine or butter
1 cup sugar
2 eggs, beaten

⅔ cup all-purpose flour
1 tsp. vanilla
dash of salt
chopped nuts

Makes 4 dozen. In a sauce pan, melt chocolate and margarine over
low heat. Add sugar, beaten eggs, flour, vanilla and salt. Spread thin
over a greased jelly roll pan. Sprinkle with chopped nuts. Bake at 350°
for 20 minutes. Cool on rack, then cut in squares.

GOOEY BARS

Candi Williams

1 box Duncan Hines devils food
cake mix
(8-oz.) cream cheese softened
1 box powdered sugar
3 eggs

1 tsp. vanilla (make sure it's a
complete teaspoon)
1 stick butter (no substitutes)
1 cup chopped pecans

Mix box of cake mix with 1 stick of butter and 1 egg. Pour into a 9 x
13 pan. In a separate bowl combine softened cream cheese, box of
powdered sugar, vanilla and pecans. Pour over the cake mixture and
bake for 40 minutes in a 350° oven.

64809B-05

HERSHEY'S BEST BROWNIES

Elaine Scales

1 cup butter
2 cups sugar
2 tsp. vanilla
4 eggs
¾ cups Hershey's cocoa

1 cup all-purpose flour
½ tsp. baking powder
¼ tsp. salt
1 cup chopped pecans

Makes 30 or more servings. Heat oven to 350°. Grease a 9 x 13 pan. Melt butter, stir in sugar and vanilla. Beat in eggs one at a time. Add cocoa, flour, baking powder and salt (after sifting together). Beat until well blended. Stir in nuts. Pour into baking dish. Bake 30 to 35 minutes.

LEMON-CHEESE CAKE BARS

Joan Hall

1 pkg. Lemon Cake mix (reg
   size)

½ cup margarine, softened
1 egg (at room temperature)

Mix all ingredients well (mixture will be coarse). Press into ungreased 9 x 13 pan.

1 (8-oz.) pkg. cream cheese
1 lb. powdered sugar or 4 cups
   unsifted

2 eggs (at room temperature)

Mix ingredients well and spread on top of mixture in 9 x 13 pan. Bake at 350° for 35 minutes (top will be slightly brown and center will be soft when done). Cool and cut into squares. Chopped nuts or coconut or both may be added to top before baking.

MELTAWAY MINT BROWNIES

Laurel Fye

1 pkg. brownie mix
water, vegetable oil and eggs as
   called for on brownie mix
   package

½ cup quartered, unwrapped
   chocolate-covered peppermint
   patties

Preheat oven to 350°. Make brownie batter according to package directions for a 9 x 13 pan. Spread ½ brownie batter into 9 x 13 pan. Sprinkle patties in single layer over batter. Spoon remaining batter over patties; spread gently to cover. Bake 25 to 30 minutes or until toothpick inserted 2-inches from side of pan comes out almost clear. Cool completely before cutting.

64809B-05

OATMEAL BROWNIES

Dee St. Laurent, Winship Volunteer
Interpreted from Weight Watchers

½ cup plus 2 T. uncooked
  oatmeal
¼ cup unsweetened applesauce
½ cup sugar
⅓ cup cocoa powder

2 tsp. salt
¼ cup honey
2 egg whites
1 tsp. vanilla extract

Makes 8 servings. Mix oatmeal and applesauce and let stand for 5 minutes. Add remaining ingredients; mix well. Spread batter in an 8-inch pan that has been sprayed with PAM. Bake a 325° for 22 minutes or until edges are dry and center is set. Cut into 8 servings. Very low in calories.

PECAN PIE SURPRISE BARS

Jane Miller, Winship Volunteer

1 pkg. yellow cake mix, divided
½ cup butter, melted

1 egg

Filling

⅔ cup cake mix
1½ cups corn syrup
3 eggs

1 cup pecans
1 tsp. vanilla extract

Makes 12 servings. Grease bottom and sides of a 13 x 9 pan. Reserve ⅔ cup of cake mix for filling. In a large bowl, combine remaining cake mix, butter and 1 egg. Mix until crumbly. Press into pan and bake at 350° for 15 to 20 minutes or until golden brown. While this bakes, mix all ingredients for filling. When cake is done, pour filling on top and bake again until filling sets--30 to 35 minutes.

64809B-05

ROCKY ROAD BROWNIES
(Gluten-Free)

Anita Janeczek
Original source: Carol Fenster-"Special Diet
Celebrations"

½ cup brown rice flour
1 lg. egg*
2 tsp. vanilla extract
¼ cup warm (105°) water or
coffee
½ cup gluten free/dairy free
chocolate free chips
½ cup chopped pecans
½ cup dried tart cherries or
cranberries
½ cup granulated sugar or
fructose powder
½ cup gluten free miniature Jet
Puff marshmallows

½ cup brown sugar or maple
sugar
½ cup potato starch
¼ cup tapioca flour
½ cup cocoa (not Dutch)
½ tsp. baking powder
½ tsp. salt
¼ tsp. xanthan gum
¼ cup butter or spectrum
cooking spray, canola oil
spread or cooking oil

Makes 12 servings. Preheat oven to 350°. Grease 8-inch square non-stick pan or spray with cooking spray. Stir together the flours, cocoa, baking powder, salt and xanthan gum (and egg replacer, if using). Set aside. In a large mixing bowl, beat the butter and sugars with an electric mixer on medium speed until well combined. Add egg and vanilla; beat until well combined. With mixer on low speed, add dry ingredients. Mix until just blended--a few lumps may remain. Gently stir in chocolate chips, nuts, marshmallows and cherries or cranberries. Spread batter in prepared pan and bake for 35 minutes or until a toothpick inserted in the center comes out clean. Cool brownies before cutting. *Omit egg and add 2 teaspoons of EnerG Egg replacer with dry ingredients.

64809B-05

This & That
(Sauces, Beverages, etc.)

Helpful Hints

- To refinish antiques or revitalize wood, use equal parts of linseed oil, white vinegar, and turpentine. Rub into the furniture or wood with a soft cloth and lots of elbow grease.

- To stop the ants in your pantry, seal off cracks where they are entering with putty or petroleum jelly. Also, try sprinkling red pepper on floors and counter tops.

- To fix sticking sliding doors, windows, and drawers, rub wax along their tracks.

- To make a simple polish for copper bottom cookware, mix equal parts of flour and salt with vinegar to create a paste. Store the paste in the refrigerator.

- Applying baking soda on a damp sponge will remove starch deposits from an iron. Make sure the iron is cold and unplugged.

- Remove stale odors in the wash by adding baking soda.

- To clean Teflon™, combine 1 cup water, 2 tablespoons baking soda and ½ cup liquid bleach. Boil in stained pan for 5 to 10 minutes or until the stain disappears. Wash, rinse, dry, and condition with oil before using the pan again.

- Corning Ware can be cleaned by filling it with water and dropping in two denture cleaning tablets. Let stand for 30 to 45 minutes.

- A little instant coffee will work wonders on your wood furniture. Just make a thick paste from instant coffee and a little water, and rub it into the nicks and scratches on your dark wood furniture. You'll be amazed at how new and beautiful those pieces will look.

- For a clogged shower head, boil it for 15 minutes in a mixture of ½ cup vinegar and 1 quart water.

- For a spicy aroma, toss dried orange or lemon rinds into the fireplace.

- Add raw rice to the salt shaker to keep the salt free-flowing.

- Ice cubes will help sharpen garbage disposal blades.

- Separate stuck-together glasses by filling the inside one with cold water and setting them in hot water.

THIS & THAT (SAUCES, BEVERAGES, ETC.)

ARRABBIATA SAUCE

Judy Baker
Interpreted from "Good Housekeeping: A Very Merry
Christmas Cookbook 2003"

½ cup extra virgin olive oil
6 garlic cloves, crushed with
  side of chef's knife
4 (35-oz.) cans Italian plum
  tomatoes

1 T. salt
1 to 1½ tsp. crushed red pepper

Makes about 14 cups. In an 8-quart Dutch oven, heat oil over medium heat until hot but not smoking. Add garlic and cook, stirring for 2 minutes; do not brown. Stir in tomatoes with their juice, salt and red pepper; heat to boiling over high heat. Reduce heat; simmer, uncovered for 50 minutes, or until sauce thickens slightly, stirring occasionally and crushing tomatoes with side of spoon. For smooth, traditional texture, press tomato mixture through food mill into large bowl. Or, leave sauce as is for a hearty, chunky texture. Cool sauce slightly. Spoon into jars. Store in refrigerator up to 1 week; or spoon into freezer-proof containers and freeze up to 2 months.

AVOCADO SALSA

Sarah Burt
Original Source: "Cooking Light" magazine

1 cup finely chopped tomato
½ cup chopped fresh cilantro
½ cup chopped peeled avocado
2 T. finely chopped red onion
3 T. fresh lime juice

¼ tsp. sea salt
1 garlic, minced
1 jalapeño pepper, seeded and
  minced

Combine all ingredients in a bowl; lightly mash with a fork.

64809B-05

BUTTERSCOTCH SAUCE

Judy Baker
Interpreted from "Good Housekeeping: A Very Merry
Christmas Cookbook 2003"

4 cups packed light brown
  sugar
2 cups heavy or whipping cream
1⅓ cups light corn syrup
½ cup butter or margarine (1
  stick)

4 tsp. distilled white vinegar
½ tsp. salt
4 tsp. vanilla extract

Makes about 6 cups. In a 5-quart Dutch oven (do not use smaller pot because mixture bubbles up during cooking), combine brown sugar, heavy cream, corn syrup, butter, vinegar and salt; heat to boiling over high heat, stirring occasionally. Reduce heat; simmer for 5 minutes, uncovered, stirring frequently. Remove Dutch oven from heat; stir in vanilla. Sauce will have thin consistency when hot but will thicken when chilled. Cool sauce completely. Transfer to jars with tight-fitting lids. Store in refrigerator up to 2 weeks. Reheat to serve warm over ice cream.

Today, I relax, let things happen and just enjoy myself.

64809B-05

CANDIED CITRUS PEEL

Judy Baker
Interpreted from "Good Housekeeping: A Very Merry
Christmas Cookbook 2003"

3 lg. grapefruit or 5 navel
  oranges

3½ cups sugar
½ cups water

Score peel of each fruit into quarters, cutting just through the rind and white pitch. Pull peel from fruit (you should have about 14 ounces of peel). Refrigerate fruit for another use. Cut grapefruit peel crosswise or orange peel lengthwise into strips about ¼-inch wide. In 4-quart saucepan, combine peel and enough water to cover; heat to boiling over high heat. Boil 5 minutes; drain. Repeat step 2 two more times, draining peel well and using fresh water each time (3 blanchings in all). In 12-inch skillet, combine 2½ cups sugar with 1½ cups water; cook over high heat, stirring constantly, until sugar dissolves and mixture boils. Boil 15 minutes, stirring occasionally (if using a candy thermometer, temperature should read 230° to 235°F). Add drained peel to syrup in skillet and stir to coat evenly. Partially covered, reduce heat and simmer for 1 hour or until peel has absorbed most of syrup, stirring occasionally. Remove cover and continue to simmer, stirring gently, until all syrup has been absorbed. On a sheet of waxed paper, place remaining 1 cup sugar. With tongs, lightly roll peel a few pieces at a time in sugar; place in single layer on wire racks. Let peel dry at least 12 hours. Dry longer if necessary; peels should be dry on the outside but still moist on the inside. Store at room temperature in airtight container up to 1 month.

64809B-05

CANDIED CUCUMBER RINGS OR STICKS

Susan Holton
Original Source: Billie Crews

8 lg. cucumbers
1 cup pickling lime
1 cup vinegar
1 T. alum
red food coloring

2 cups water
2 cups vinegar
8 cups sugar
1 (8-oz.) bag "red hot" candies

Makes 3 to 4 pints. Peel cucumbers and cut in ½-inch round slices or sticks. Remove seeds. Soak in 1 gallon of water and 1 cup lime for 24 hours. Drain; mix vinegar, alum and food coloring. Add cucumbers and enough water to cover and simmer for two hours. Drain. Make syrup using 2 cups water and 2 cups vinegar, sugar and cinnamon candies. Add cucumbers to mixture and bring to a boil. Remove from heat and let stand overnight. Heat cucumbers in syrup; pack in hot sterilized jars and seal.

CINNAMON PECANS

Lynn Gibson

3 cups pecans
1 cup sugar
1 tsp. cinnamon

1 tsp. salt
1 tsp. vanilla
5 T. water

Makes 6 servings. Toast pecans on a cookie sheet in a 300° oven for 5 minutes. Place the remaining ingredients in a large saucepan over high heat. Put top on pan until mixture comes to a rolling boil. Then take the cover off and let it cook 1½ minutes. Pour in the pecans and stir until all liquid is absorbed. Pour pecans onto wax paper and separate them with a spoon to dry.

64809B-05

CRISP SWEET CUCUMBER PICKLES

Jean Scruggs

Spice bag

1 tsp. celery seed   1 tsp. all spice
1 tsp. cinnamon   1 tsp. ginger

Syrup

5 lbs. sugar   3 pts. apple cider vinegar

Makes 7 pints. Peel 7 pounds yellow or large cucumbers (weight before preparing) and cut in strips--be sure cucumbers are very large. Cut out centers (seeds). Soak for 24 hours in 3 cups lime mixed in 2 gallons of water. Then change water every hour for 4 hours. Soak cucumbers in syrup overnight. Then bring to a boil; reduce to simmer for 1 hour. Put spices in small square of cotton cloth and tie. Place in syrup while cooking. Remove spice bag, put pickles in a jar and seal. For a zestier flavor, add 1 pod hot green pepper to each jar before sealing.

ESSENSEPAULA'S SOFT SPIRIT FRUIT WINE

Paula Cook-Thompson, Winship Volunteer

1 or more peaches   ¼ or more banana
10 or more grapes   3 or more ice cubes

Let fruit sit in a closed plastic container or jar; room temperature for 3 days until ripe. Blend to your desired texture. Or you can: Let fruit sit in a closed plastic container in the refrigerator for 7 days until it gets a little riper. Blend to your desired texture.

HOT MULLED CRANBERRY CIDER

April Leach

1 (32-oz.) jar cranberry juice   6 cinnamon sticks (8 inches
  cocktail (4 cups)   each)
1 (32-oz.) jar apple juice (4 cups)
6 tea bags (cinnamon-apple
  herbal)

Makes 6 servings. In a 3-quart saucepan over high heat, heat cranberry and apple juices. Bring to a boil. Remove from heat and add tea bags. Cover and brew 5 minutes. Remove tea bags; use cinnamon sticks as swizzle sticks in cups.

64809B-05

MARIAN'S SALAD DRESSING

Marian Stevens

1 cup canola oil
$^{1}/_{4}$ cup vinegar
$^{1}/_{2}$ tsp. dry mustard
$^{1}/_{2}$ tsp. celery seed salt

$^{1}/_{2}$ tsp. black pepper
1 tsp. (rounded) sugar
2 tsp. (rounded) salt
1 tsp. Worcestershire sauce

Mix all the ingredients together. I double this and keep in a quart jar in the refrigerator.

MARINATED OLIVES

Judy Baker
Interpreted from "Good Housekeeping: A Very Merry Christmas Cookbook 2003"

$^{1}/_{4}$ cup extra virgin olive oil
2 tsp. fennel seeds, crushed
4 sm. bay leaves
2 lbs. assorted Mediterranean olives (such as nicoise, picholine, Kalamata, and oil-cured)

6 strips (3 x 1 each) lemon peel
4 garlic cloves, crushed with side of chef's knife

Makes about 6 cups. In a 1-quart saucepan, heat oil, fennel seeds and bay leaves over medium heat until hot but not smoking. Remove saucepan from heat; let stand 10 minutes. In a large bowl, combine olive-oil mixture with olives, lemon peel and garlic. Cover bowl and refrigerate olives at least 24 hours to allow flavors to develop, stirring occasionally. (Or, in large zip-tight plastic bag, combine all ingredients, turning to coat olives well. Seal bag, pressing out as much air as possible. Place on plate; refrigerate, turning bag occasionally). Spoon olives into jars for gift giving. Store in refrigerator up to 1 month.

64809B-05

MILLION ISLAND DRESSING

Bobbie Melton

1 cup mayonnaise
¼ cup chili sauce
1½ tsp. Worcestershire sauce
12 stuffed olives

1 med. onion sliced ¼ inch
   thick
2 med. dill pickles cut in slices
2 hard-boiled eggs, quartered

Put first 3 ingredients in a blender. Process on medium speed, until well blended. Add remaining ingredients and process on chop--don't chop too much because true Million Island Dressing is coarse and lumpy.

ORANGE JULIUS

Kathy Fonder

½ of a 6-oz. can of frozen
   orange juice concentrate
½ cup milk
½ cup water

¼ cup sugar
½ tsp. vanilla
5-6 cubes ice (or more)

Combine all ingredients in a blender. Blend on high and serve.

PARTY PUNCH

Nikki Elliott

(12-oz.) can frozen orange juice
(12-oz.) can frozen lemonade
1 lg. can unsweetened
   pineapple juice

6 cups water
1 cup sugar

Makes 12 servings. Mix together and freeze. When ready to serve, use ice pick or fork to break up frozen punch. Add to punch bowl with 1.5 liters ginger ale.

I cross the bridges of change with joy and ease.

64809B-05

PARTY PUNCH-VARIATION 2

Dorothy Ford

4 cups water
2 cups sugar
(46-oz.) can unsweetened
  pineapple juice

4 lg. or 6 medium bananas
2 (28-oz.) bottles ginger ale or
  7-Up (room temperature)

Makes 12 servings. Boil water and sugar until dissolved; cool. In blender, purée lemonade, pineapple juice and bananas. Mix everything together and pour into plastic container; freeze. Remove from freezer at least 3 hours before serving. Place in punch bowl and break into large chunks with spoon. Add ginger ale or 7-Up. Serve.

PUMPKIN DIP

Claire Smith

4 cups confectioner's sugar,
  sifted
2 (8-oz.) pkgs. cream cheese,
  softened

1 (16-oz.) can solid pack
  pumpkin
2 tsp. cinnamon
1 tsp. ginger

Combine confectioner's sugar, cream cheese, pumpkin, cinnamon and ginger. Serve with ginger snaps or pumpkin bread. "I hollow out a small pumpkin and serve the pumpkin dip in the pumpkin."

SESAME SAUCE

Debbie Foster, Winship Volunteer

1 sm. or ½ medium tomato
  peeled, seeded and coarsely
  chopped--about ½ a cup
3 T. soy sauce
3 T. red wine vinegar
2 T. dark sesame oil
1 T. chopped fresh chives

1 T. small piece fresh ginger,
  peeled and finely chopped
2 cloves garlic (1 tsp. minced)
1 tsp. sugar
1 tsp. sesame seeds
¼ tsp. ground black pepper

Sauté ginger and garlic in sesame seed oil and add other ingredients; heat thoroughly. Remove from heat and use over room temperature asparagus.

64809B-05

SUMMER SLUSH RECIPE

Jane Miller, Winship Volunteer

2 regular-size tea bags
1 cup hot water
1 cup sugar
3½ cups water

1 can (med size) frozen orange juice
1 can frozen lemonade

Makes 5 servings. Brew 2 regular-size tea bags in 1 cup of hot water. Dissolve 1 cup of sugar in hot water. Add 3½ cups water, 1 can frozen orange juice and 1 can frozen lemonade. Stir in container and freeze.

TOMATO GRAVY

Linda Appleton

4 T. unsalted butter or bacon drippings
4 T. all-purpose flour
2 cups milk, heated
salt and freshly ground pepper to taste

1 clove garlic, minced
6 med. ripe tomatoes, peeled, cored, cut into eighths or 1 28 oz. can tomatoes

Makes 8 servings. Melt butter or drippings in skillet over medium-high heat. Add flour and whisk constantly until light brown. Whisk in warm milk and bring to a boil. Season with salt and pepper and add garlic. Reduce heat, add tomatoes; simmer slowly until tomatoes are soft and integrated into gravy. Serve over hot biscuits.

Recipe Favorites

64809B-05

Recipe Favorites

64809B-05

Eating Well
Through Cancer

What Cancer Cannot Do

Cancer is so limited

It cannot cripple love

It cannot shatter hope

It cannot corrode faith

It cannot eat away peace

It cannot destroy confidence

It cannot kill friendship

It cannot shut our memories

It cannot silence courage

It cannot invade the soul

It cannot reduce eternal life

It cannot quench the spirit

Author Unknown

EATING WELL THROUGH CANCER

APPLE AND PRUNE SAUCE

Tiffany Barrett, Nutrition Specialist
Original Source: National Institutes of Health

⅓ cup unprocessed bran   ⅓ cup mashed stewed prunes
⅓ cup applesauce

Blend all ingredients and store in the refrigerator. Take 1 to 2 tablespoons then drink 8 ounces of water. Use this recipe to relieve constipation. Contains 10 calories per 1 tablespoon

BANANA OAT SHAKE

Tiffany Barrett, Nutrion Specialist

⅓ to ½ cup cooked oatmeal,   1 T. wheat germ
  chilled   1 T. honey
1 banana (frozen if thicker   1 tsp. vanilla extract
  smoothie is desired)
1 cup milk (may substitute
  Ensure, Boost, etc.)

Blend all ingredients until smooth. Contains: 425 calories; 16 g protein; 4 g fat

Health experts widely believe that obtaining the proper nutrients from whole foods is more effective than obtaining them from supplements. A single fruit or vegetable may contain scores of nutrients and beneficial chemicals that are missing in a supplement.

64809B-05

BEAN SOUP

Tiffany Barrett, Nutrition Specialist

2 (12 or 15-oz.) cans white
   beans, drained
2 T. olive oil
1 med. onion, finely chopped
2 lg. carrots, peeled and
   chopped
1 stalk celery, chopped
2 cloves garlic, minced

1 tsp. minced, fresh rosemary (if
   fresh is not available, try ½ to
   1 tsp. ground, dried rosemary)
7 to 8 cups vegetable stock
salt and pepper to taste
¼ cup fresh grated Parmesan
   cheese
2 T. chopped fresh parsley

Makes 4 servings. Rinsing away the liquid around canned beans can help cut down on the amount of gas you may experience from beans. In a large pot, warm the olive oil over medium-high heat. Add onion, carrot, and celery. Sauté while stirring lightly until vegetables are soft (5 to 10 minutes). Add garlic & rosemary and sauté for another 3 to 4 minutes. Add drained beans and vegetable stock. Bring to a boil, reduce heat, and simmer gently for 20 to 30 minutes. After simmering, place ⅓ to ½ of the bean soup in the blender. Blend until thick & smooth. Be careful when blending, letting steam and heat escape every few seconds, by lifting blender lid slowly throughout blending. If steam & heat build up, the lid can blow off the blender. Return blended soup to pot and stir to mix. Season with salt & pepper. Garnish with Parmesan and parsley. Each serving contains: 325 calories, 16 g protein, 9 g fat, 10 g fiber

COFFEE MILK SHAKE

Tiffany Barrett, Nutrition Specialist

1 cup vanilla ice cream
1 pkg. vanilla Carnation Instant
   Breakfast

(4-oz.) half and half milk
1 pkg. instant coffee (dissolved
   in 1 T. hot water)

Blend until desired consistency. Contains: 559 calories, 15 g fat

64809B-05

CRANBERRY APPLE SALAD

Tiffany Barrett, Nutrition Specialist

1½ cups chopped cranberries
  (fresh or dried)
1 cup apple, chopped
1 cup celery, chopped
1 cup seedless grapes, halved
⅓ cup raisins

¼ cup walnuts, chopped
2 T. sugar (or other sweetener)
¼ tsp. cinnamon
1 (8-oz.) carton vanilla nonfat
  yogurt

Makes 9 servings. Mix all ingredients together. Cover and chill for at least two hours. Each serving contains: 78 calories, 1.5 g fiber, 1.6 g fat

CREAM OF BROCCOLI SOUP

Tiffany Barrett, Nutrition Specialist

2 cups whole or high protein
  milk
2 T. flour
2 T. margarine, melted

1 tsp. salt
dash pepper to taste
1 cup cooked broccoli
1 T. onion, diced and cooked

Makes 4 servings. Mix all the ingredients in a blender. This is the base for all the soups. Blend with broccoli or other vegetables (i.e. peas or carrots). Heat until thickened and serve. Each serving of the base contains: 200 calories, 5 g protein

Try to resume your normal, day-to-day activities as soon as possible. Thirty minutes of moderate activity every day (such as walking), even if done in three 10-minute bursts, will make more energetic and healthier. Consult your doctor before taking up a more vigorous exercise routine.

64809B-05

GRILLED SALMON WITH DILL SAUCE

Tiffany Barrett, Nutrition Specialist

1 lb. salmon fillets
2 cups white wine
¼ tsp. pepper

¼ tsp. salt
1 tsp. dried dill

Sauce

⅓ cup light or fat free mayo
1 T. ketchup
¼ tsp. Worcestershire sauce
¼ tsp. soy sauce
2 drops hot sauce

1 tsp. lemon juice
1 tsp. dried dill
1 tsp. dried parsley
1 garlic clove, minced

Makes 4 servings. Cut fillets into four pieces and marinate in wine for 1 hour in the refrigerator. Mix all the ingredients for dill sauce and chill. Sprinkle dry ingredients over fillets and rub in on both sides. Grill on hot skillet for 3 to 5 minutes on each side. Sprinkle with lemon juice as fillets cook. Each serving contains: 250 calories, 12 g fat, 2.5 g sat fat, 4 g monounsaturated fat

HIGH PROTEIN MILK

Tiffany Barrett, Nutrition Specialist

1 cup whole milk

4 T. dry milk powder

Makes 1 cup. Add dry milk and beat until dissolved. Serve cold. Use with cereals, cream sauces, mashed potatoes, soups, pancakes, etc. Contains: 270 calories, 14 g protein

ORANGE FANTASY

Tiffany Barrett, Nutrion Specialist

¼ cup lemonade
¼ cup orange juice

½ cup whole milk
½ cup orange sherbet

Mix together thoroughly. This is a tart drink (not recommended if you have mouth sores). Contains: 365 calories, 6 g protein

64809B-05

POWER MILK SHAKE

Tiffany Barrett, Nutrion Specialist

1 cup ice cream
1 env. Carnation Instant
Breakfast or Nonfat Dry Milk
Powder

1/2 cup whole milk
1/2 cup fresh, frozen, or canned
fruit
3 T. peanut butter

Combine all ingredients in a blender and mix until smooth. Freeze any portion not taken for later use. Contains: 575 calories, 21 g protein

RASPBERRY DELIGHT

Tiffany Barrett, Nutrion Specialist

1 cup raspberry yogurt or
sherbet

1/2 cup half and half
1/4 cup cranberry juice

Mix together thoroughly. This is a tart drink (not recommended if you have mouth sores). Contains: 430 calories, 12 g protein

SAUTÉED SPINACH

Tiffany Barrett, Nutrition Specialist

1 tsp. olive oil
1 1/2 cups sliced mushrooms
1 Vidalia onion, sliced
2 cloves garlic, sliced

1 pkg. fresh spinach
1/2 tsp. minced ginger
2 tsp. soy sauce

Makes 4 servings. In a medium saucepan over low, heat olive oil. Add mushrooms, onions and garlic. Sauté 15 to 20 minutes or until onions and mushrooms are soft. Add spinach, ginger and soy sauce. Cover and cook until spinach is wilted. Each serving contains: 62 calories, 1.5 g fat

STRAWBERRY SMOOTHIE

Tiffany Barrett, Nutrition Specialist

1/2 cup strawberries or other
fruit

1/2 cup high protein milk
1/2 tsp. vanilla

Blend fruit, add all ingredients until thoroughly blended. Serve chilled. Add sugar for extra sweetness. Contains: 200 calories, 7 g protein

64809B-05

Recipe Favorites

64809B-05

Nutrition during Cancer Treatment

Recommendations for cancer patients during treatment can vary over time. Throughout the phases of cancer treatment and recovery, it is important to adapt what you eat to cope with your body's changing needs. Nutrition for cancer patients may focus on high calorie and protein foods. Side effects of cancer treatment vary from each patient and vary during the treatment phase.

Coping with Eating Problems

The following suggestions may help you cope with eating problems. Try these ideas to find what works best for you.

Nausea

If nausea becomes a problem, you might start to associate the foods you eat during treatment with feeling of nauseated or tired.

- Eat several small meals each day instead of a few large ones.
- Some people find that keeping a little food in their stomach can help prevent nausea. Even a bite or two can help. Do not let your stomach get completely empty.
- Try dry toast, crackers, etc. in the morning before you eat breakfast.
- Keep snacks handy to eat immediately. Try bland, dry, salty foods such as pretzels or crackers.
- Eat foods cold or at room temperature to prevent intolerance to strong smells. Avoid very sweet, fried, greasy, spicy foods or foods with strong odors.

- Chew food well and slowly.
- Suck on mints or hard candies.
- Drink cool, clear, unsweetened juices (exp. apple or grape juice) or decaffeinated sodas (sprite, ginger ale).
- Drink and sip on fluids during the day rather than with meals. Fluids can increase fullness.
- Aim for 6 to 8 cups of fluids a day.

- Ginger may relieve nausea; try ginger root, or sipping ginger tea.
- Avoid eating 1 to 2 hours before treatment if nausea occurs during radiation or chemotherapy.
- Avoid lying down for at least 2 hours after meals.
- Wear loose fitting clothing
- Pay attention to when nausea occurs and possible causes. You may need to change your diet around your treatment schedule.

Vomiting

- Do not try to eat or drink anything until the vomiting is under control.
- Once vomiting is under control, try small amounts of clear liquids and gradually work up to a regular diet.

Appetite Loss

Loss of appetite is a common problem with cancer and cancer treatment. Many things contribute to poor appetite including nausea, vomiting, change in taste or smell or change in emotions. It is very important that you eat enough to keep your weight up during treatment. Keeping your weight up will help you tolerate your treatments better and heal faster. You can use the following tips to make sure you eat enough.

- Eat several small meals throughout the day, keep snacks handy, and drink liquid supplements/milkshakes when you don't feel like eating solid foods.
- Do not wait until you are hungry to eat. Even if you eat a couple of bites every hour.
- Treat food like medication: Set specific times to eat, such as every 1 or 2 hours. Drink 2-4 oz of liquid supplement with medications.
- Make sure what you are eating is packed with calories and protein.

- Add extra protein and calories to your diet. Use fortified milk by adding 1 cup nonfat dry milk to 1 QT whole milk.
- Add fruit, flavorings, peanut butter, etc to liquid supplements such as Boost and Ensure.
- Eat your favorite foods anytime of the day.
- Recognize that family and friends want to help you. Do not force yourself to eat when you feel poorly.

Good Snacks:

Cheese and crackers
Yogurt, pudding
Nuts, peanut butter, dried fruit
Cheese
Popcorn
Canned tuna, chicken
Trail Mix
Milkshakes, smoothies, instant breakfast

Sore Mouth and Throat

Discuss the reason for the soreness with your doctor, use medication if prescribed and eat soft foods that are easy to chew and swallow. Avoid foods that are tart, spicy, salty, or crunchy.

- Focus on soft and liquid foods. These are easier to eat and this can help you eat better, even if your mouth hurts.
- Eat soft, bland foods such as creamed soup, casseroles, eggs, mashed potatoes, oatmeal or cream of wheat, pasta, bananas, canned peaches or pears, yogurt, cottage cheese, and pudding.
- Puree or liquefy foods in a blender to make them smoother.
- Eat foods cold or at room temperature. Hot foods can irritate a tender mouth.
- Avoid acidic, spicy or salty foods (exp. tomatoes, citrus, chili powder, salsa, etc.)

- Take small bites and use a straw for liquids.
- Rinse your mouth often with baking soda mouthwash to remove food and germs.
- Add broth, gravies, sauces, or soup to moisten and soften food.
- Try sucking on frozen fruit and ice chips.
- Use olive oil or canola oil to make foods slippery.

Dry Mouth

Dry mouth and thick saliva can be a problem for some individuals undergoing cancer treatment. If you are having trouble eating because you have a dry mouth or thick saliva try the following tips.

- Sip on water throughout the day (carry a water bottle everywhere).
- When eating, take small bites and chew food completely.
- Eat soft, moist foods that are cool or at room temperature.
- Try soft cooked chicken and fish, thinned cereals, popsicles, shakes, smoothies and slushies; warm soups and stews.
- Add broth, sauces, gravy, or soup to soften and moisten foods.
- Try canned fruit which is soft, plus it is already in liquid, making it easier to swallow.
- Suck on popsicles, ice chips, and sugar free hard candy.
- Try tart or sweet foods such as lemonade.
- Use salad dressings to make food slippery (on salads or vegetables etc.)

Changes in Taste and Smell

Sometimes during cancer treatment your sense of taste or smell may change. Some foods, especially meat, may have a metallic taste. Here are some tips that may help with intake if you have this problem:

- Choose and prepare foods that look and smell good to you.
- Look for foods with a stronger flavor (exp. chocolate is stronger than vanilla).
- Try tart or spicy foods unless the mouth or throat is sore.
- Use plastic silverware to reduce metallic taste and avoid drinking out of soft drink cans or other metallic containers.
- Try cold or room temperature foods that have less taste or aroma.
- Sip on ginger ale, lemon juice or suck on hard candy to offset bad taste.
- If red meat taste or smells bad, try chicken, turkey, dairy or mild tasting fish instead.
- Help the flavor of meat by marinating it in fruit juices, Italian dressing, sweet and sour sauce, etc.
- Try using small amounts of flavorful seasonings.

Diarrhea

Diarrhea can be caused from chemotherapy, radiation, infection, food sensitivities, and emotional upset.

- Increase intake of foods high in soluble fiber such as oatmeal, white rice, bananas, white toast, applesauce, canned fruits (avoid the skins and peels of fruit), pasta, and cream of rice cereal.
- Decrease intake of foods high in insoluble fiber, such as fresh fruit with the peel, raw vegetables, whole grain breads and cereals, beans, peas, and popcorn.
- Avoid fatty, fried and spicy foods
- Drink 6 to 8 cups of fluids each day. Let carbonated beverages lose their fizz before drinking.
- Limit foods that contain caffeine, such as coffee, chocolate and some sodas.

- Drink fluids at room temperature.
- Drink broth and sports drinks to replace electrolyte losses.
- Try non-acidic juices, such as apricot nectar, peach nectar, or pear nectar.

Constipation

- Drink plenty of liquids. Hot beverages and juices (exp. prunes) are often effective.
- Eat high fiber foods: bran, whole grain breads and cereals, raw and cooked vegetables, nuts, fresh and dried fruit.
- If possible, try increasing physical activity, even a small amount. Try taking a short walk about one hour before your normal time for a bowel movement.
- Check with your doctor before taking any laxatives or stool softeners.

Safe Food Handling Tips

These guidelines are intended to minimize the introduction of bacteria for immunosuppressed patients. Neutropenic patients may require more strict precautions.

- Wash hands very well before any food preparation.
- Wash all fruits and vegetables thoroughly. If it can't be washed well avoid it. Scrub tough melons prior to cutting.
- Thaw meat in the refrigerator, not on the kitchen counter.
- Be sure to cook meat and eggs thoroughly.
- Use only pasteurized juices and dairy products
- Sanitize all food preparation surfaces (plastic cutting board, knives, utensils, counter top).
- Avoid food with visible mold (includes aged cheeses)
- Avoid all miso products
- Pay close attention to expiration dates.

Weight Gain

Discuss the reason for the weight gain with your physician. Some causes may include drug side effects, water retention and increased appetite. With your doctor's approval, you may want to try a lower-fat, reduced-calorie diet.

- Emphasize fruits and vegetables
- Choose lean meats
- Use low fat dairy products
- Cut back on added sweets, butter, oils, etc.
- Choose low fat cooking methods (baking, steaming, broiling)

Vitamins and Supplements

Some vitamins, minerals, and supplements can interfere with the effects of chemotherapy. To be on the safe side, check with your oncologist and healthcare team about any vitamin, supplement, or mineral you take. Remember that healthy foods can provide vitamins and minerals your body needs.

Many unproven dietary treatments do not provide enough calories and protein. This can cause unwanted weight loss, tiredness and decrease your immune function. Before making any changes to your diet, consider the following:

1. Does the diet have foods from each of the five food groups?
2. Can you stay at a healthy weight while you are on a diet?
3. Does the diet interfere with your medical treatment?
4. Are the doses of vitamins and minerals toxic to the body?
5. Does the diet claim to have unrealistic results?
6. The changes you make should be for the better. Talk about any dietary changes with your dietitian or doctor first.

After Cancer Treatment

Most nutrition related side effects go away after cancer treatment ends. When you are feeling better, you can start changing to the traditional guidelines for healthy eating. Eating right will help you regain your strength and rebuild tissue. Although factors other than diet can play a role in the development of cancer, health experts know that paying attention to diet and related factors (including body weight and exercise) is one of the most effective ways to reduce cancer risk. Research in this field is ongoing, and scientists are just beginning to sort out the complex relationships between specific food components and their various health effects.

The following are dietary guidelines set by the American Cancer Society and the American Institute of Cancer. These dietary recommendations are consistent with prevention of other diseases, including heart disease and diabetes.

- Eat a plant-based diet high in fruits, vegetables, whole grains and legumes
- Eat at least five servings of fruits and vegetables every day
- Limit your intake of red meat
- Limit your intake of fat, especially saturated (animal-based) fats
- Limit your consumption of alcohol, if you drink at all
- Eat a variety of fruits, vegetables and starchy plant foods (such as rice and pasta)

A well-balanced diet is the best nutritional approach.

INDEX OF RECIPES

APPETIZERS

BLACK BEAN SALSA 1
BLUE CHEESE DIP 1
CINNAMON TORTILLA CRISPS
AND FRUIT SALSA 2
CRAB MUFFINS APPETIZER 2
DELI APPETIZER 3
FILIPINO EGG ROLLS "LUMPIA" 3
FRUIT DIP 4
GOAT CHEESE SPREAD 4
HAM ROLLS 4
HAM ROLLUPS 5
HOLIDAY CHEESE BALL 5
HOLIDAY QUESADILLAS 6
HOT CRAB DIP 6
HOT SPINACH APPETIZER DIP 7
JANET'S SAUSAGE STARS 7
MINIATURE TOMATO
SANDWICHES 8
ORIENTAL BEEF 8
PIZZA FONDUE 9
PLAINS SPECIAL CHEESE
RING 9
RASPBERRY/PECAN BAKED
BRIE 9
SALMON PARTY LOG 10
SHRIMP (OR FRANKS) IN
DEVIL SAUCE 10
SOURDOUGH BREAD DIP 10
SPINACH FUDGE 11

SOUPS, SALADS & BREADS

SOUPS

BROCCOLI/CHEESE SOUP 13
BUTTERNUT SQUASH SOUP 13
CHICKEN SOUP 14
CHICKEN TORTILLA SOUP 14
CREAM OF BROCCOLI SOUP 15
FIESTA SOUP 15
FRENCH COUNTRY STEW 15
HARVEST BISQUE 16
KIELBASA STEW 16
LIGURIAN MINESTONE 17
MEDITERRANEAN SEAFOOD
STEW 18
MUGSY'S HOT AND SOUR
SOUP 18
POOR MAN'S VEGGIE SOUP 19
POTATO BACON CHOWDER 19
SAUSAGE BEAN CHOWDER 19
SAUSAGE CORN CHOWDER 20

SAVORY BEEF AND
VEGETABLE STEW 20
UNBELIEVABLE BEEF BARLEY
SOUP 21
YUMMY POTATO SOUP 22

SALADS

ANTIPASTO SALAD 22
BROCCOLI BACON SALAD 23
BROCCOLI SLAW 23
CAESAR SLAW 24
CARROT SALAD 24
CHICKEN SALAD 24
COBB LANE CHICKEN SALAD 25
CURRIED CHICKEN AND RICE
SALAD 25
GERMAN POTATO SALAD 26
GREEN-&-GOLD SALAD WITH
FRESH CITRUS RANCH
DRESSING 26
HOT CHICKEN SALAD 27
MACARONI SALAD 27
MANDARIN SALAD 28
MEDITERRANEAN PASTA
SALAD 28
MEXICAN SALAD 29
MYSTERY SALAD 29
NO FAIL POTATO SALAD 29
ORIENTAL CHICKEN SALAD 30
SAUERKRAUT SALAD 30
SHRIMP SALAD 30
TABBOULEH (LEBANESE
BULGUR SALAD) 31

BREADS

APPLE MUFFINS 32
BAKED FRENCH TOAST 32
BANANA BREAD 33
BANANA BREAD 33
BASIL BISCUITS 34
BLUEBERRY BANANA LOAF 34
BLUEBERRY QUICK BREAD 35
BRUSCHETTA 35
CAST-IRON SWEET
CORNBREAD 36
CHEESY BREAD 36
CINNAMON BREAD 37
CORN MUFFINS 37
CRANBERRY BREAD 38
CREAM CHEESE BRAIDS 38
IRISH SODA BREAD 39
JUDY'S CHEDDAR CHEESE
BREAD 39
MARLA'S POPPY SEED CAKE
BREAD 39

MOIST PUMPKIN BREAD	40	
PARMESAN MONKEY BREAD	40	
PEAR BREAD	40	
PINEAPPLE BANANA LOAF	41	
PINEAPPLE ZUCCHINI LOAF	41	
PLUM BREAD	42	
PUMPKIN LOAF	42	
RAISIN BRAN MUFFINS	43	
RAISIN LOAF	43	
RHUBARB LOAF	44	
ROSEMARY-FENNEL BREADSTICKS	44	
ST. JOHN'S BANANA BREAD	45	
"SWEETNESS BISCUITS"	31	
ZUCCHINI BREAD	45	

VEGETABLES & SIDE DISHES

VEGETABLES

BAKED CORN	47
BAKED VIDALIA ONIONS	47
BASIL BUTTERED BEANS	47
CABBAGE AND NOODLES (HUNGARIAN STYLE)	48
CAULIFLOWER MOUNTAIN	48
CORN PUDDING	48
CREAMED SPINACH	49
EGGPLANT PARMESAN	49
EGGPLANT, RED PEPPER, AND FETA GRATIN	50
FIVE-VEGETABLE MEDLEY	50
FREEZER FRESH CREAMED CORN	51
GLAZED CARROTS	51
GREEN BEANS WITH HONEY-PECAN BUTTER	52
IMPOSSIBLE GARDEN PIE	52
LEMONY BRUSSELS SPROUTS	53
MARINATED VEGETABLES	53
ONION PUDDING	54
RITZ SQUASH CASSEROLE	54
ROASTED ASPARAGUS	54
ROASTED CARROTS WITH BALSAMIC VINEGAR	55
ROASTED VEGETABLES	55
SAVORY MUSHROOM CUSTARD	55
SCALLOPED CORN	56
SHOE PEG CORN	56
SPINACH CASSEROLE	57
SPINACH ZUCCHINI POTATO PANCAKES	57
SQUASH CASSEROLE	57
TEXAS SCALLOPED CORN	58
TOMATO PIE	58

ZUCCHINI WITH CITRUS-HERB DRESSING	59

SIDE DISHES

BAKED ALL THE BEANS	60
BAKED MACARONI AND CHEESE (WITH OR WITHOUT HAM)	60
BEANS, PASTA, AND GREENS	61
DEVILED EGGS	61
EASY MACARONI AND CHEESE	62
FRIED RICE	62
GARLIC GRITS	62
PARTYTIME BAKED BEANS	63
PEG'S SWEET POTATO CASSEROLE	63
PINEAPPLE CASSEROLE I	64
PINEAPPLE CASSEROLE II	64
POTATO CASSEROLE	64
RATATOUILLE	65
RICE WITH PEAS	65
ROSEMARY POTATOES	66
SWEET POTATO CASSEROLE	66
"THE BEST BAKED BEANS"	59

ENTREES AND CASSEROLES

ENTREES

ARMENIAN MEAT PIZZA	67
BAKED CHICKEN BREASTS AND RICE	68
BAKED SWISS CHICKEN	68
BASQUE CHICKEN	69
BREAKFAST PIZZA	69
BRISKET	70
BROILED CHILEAN SEA BASS WITH SMASHED CAULIFLOWER	70
CAVITINI	71
CHEESE BISCUIT SKILLET	71
CHICKEN CACCIATORE	72
CHICKEN ITALIANO	72
CHICKEN PARISIENNE	73
CHICKEN TETRAZZINI	73
CHILI BEAN NACHO SKILLET	74
CLASSIC BEEF STROGANOFF	74
EASY LASAGNA	75
EASY PARMESAN GARLIC CHICKEN	75
FAMILY FLANK STEAK	76
GLAZED HAM	76
GREEK STEAK PITAS WITH DILL SAUCE	77

GREEK STYLE SCAMPI	77
GRILLED PORK TENDERLOIN	78
HEARTY CHICKEN BAKE	78
HONEY CHICKEN	79
ISLAND SPICE SALMON	79
LASAGNA	79
MANDARIN ORANGE CHICKEN	80
MAPLE-APPLE PORK SLICES	80
MEAT LOAF	81
MEAT LOAF FLORENTINE	81
MEAT LOAF WITH SUN-DRIED TOMATOES AND HERBS	82
MEDITERRANEAN CHICKEN	83
MEDITERRANEAN-STYLE BEEF TURNOVERS	83
MEXICAN WHITE CHILI	84
PARMESAN PEPPER MEATBALLS	84
PASTA E FAGIOLI	85
PORK CHOP SKILLET MEAL	85
RED SNAPPER VERACRUZ	86
SHANNON'S CHICKEN	86
SHRIMP PASTA	87
SHRIMP PRIMAVERA	87
SLOPPY JOES	87
SOUR CREAM ENCHILADAS	88
SPICY PORK TENDERLOIN	88
SPINACH, GARLIC, AND CHICKEN PASTA	90
SPINACH PORK TENDERLOIN	89
SPINACH TOFU QUICHE	90
STICKY CHICKEN	91
STIR FRY SHRIMP	91
STUFFED MUSHROOMS	91
STUFFED TOMATOES	92
SWEET 'N' SOUR TURKEY	92
TERIYAKI STEAK	93
TUNA STEAK ON WHITE BEANS WITH TOMATO COULIS	93
TURKEY SLOPPY JOE	94
UPSIDE DOWN PIZZA PIE	94

CASSEROLES

BAKED BLINTZ CASSEROLE	95
BREAKFAST CASSEROLE	95
BROCCOLI CASSEROLE	96
CHEESY CHICKEN AND RICE CASSEROLE	96
CHICKEN CASSEROLE	97
CHICKEN CRESCENT DINNER	97
CHICKEN POT PIE	97
CHUCK WAGON CASSEROLE	98
DINNER IN ONE CASSEROLE	98
HAMBURGER PIE	99
LAYERED CHICKEN ENCHILADA CASSEROLE	99
SMOKED SALMON BREAKFAST CASSEROLE	100

SWEETS AND DESSERTS

ALMOND TORTE	101
ANGEL SUPREME	101
BANANA PUDDING	102
BLUEBERRY YUM YUM	102
CREAM CHEESE SQUARES	103
CUBAN FLAN	103
GRANDMA'S CREAMY RICE PUDDING	104
HEAVENLY HASH	104
MOM'S FUDGE	104
PEACH FLOATING ISLAND	105
POOR MAN'S CUPCAKE	105
PUMPKIN SQUARES	106
RICE KRISPIES SCOTCHAROOS	106
STRAWBERRY SUPREME MOLD	106

CAKES

APPLESAUCE CAKE	107
BLACK FOREST DUMP CAKE	107
CAKE WITH PEANUT BUTTER FROSTING	108
CHOCOLATE CHEESECAKE	109
CHOCOLATE CHIP CAKE	110
CHOCOLATE-AMARETTO LAYER CAKE	110
CREAM CHEESE POUND CAKE	111
DATE NUT CAKE	111
FUDGEY PECAN CAKE	112
JEWISH APPLE CAKE	112
KEY LIME CAKE	113
LAYERS OF DELIGHT	114
LEMONADE CAKE	115
MILLION DOLLAR POUND CAKE	115
ORANGE CARROT CAKE	116
ORANGE SLICE CAKE	116
PINA COLADA CHEESECAKE	117
PUMPKIN SPICE CHEESECAKE	118
RUM CAKE	119

PIES

CHERRY-BERRY PEACH PIE	119
COOKIE PIE	120
GERMAN CHOCOLATE PIE	120
LEMON PIE	120
SWEET POTATO PIE	121

COOKIES

CHOCOLATE CHIP COOKIES	121

CHOCOLATE CHIP PUDDING
  COOKIES 122
CHOCOLATE COVERED OREO
  BALLS 123
CRISP SUGAR COOKIES 123
GINGER MOLASSES COOKIES 124
LEMON SQUARES 124
NANA QUEHL'S MOLASSES
  COOKIES 125
OREO DESSERT 125
SPICE COOKIES 126

CRANBERRY APPLE SALAD 143
CREAM OF BROCCOLI SOUP 143
GRILLED SALMON WITH DILL
  SAUCE 144
HIGH PROTEIN MILK 144
ORANGE FANTASY 144
POWER MILK SHAKE 145
RASPBERRY DELIGHT 145
SAUTÉED SPINACH 145
STRAWBERRY SMOOTHIE 145

BARS & BROWNIES

CHOCOLATE NUT WAFERS 127
GOOEY BARS 127
HERSHEY'S BEST BROWNIES 128
LEMON-CHEESE CAKE BARS 128
MELTAWAY MINT BROWNIES 128
OATMEAL BROWNIES 129
PECAN PIE SURPRISE BARS 129
ROCKY ROAD BROWNIES 130

THIS & THAT (SAUCES, BEVERAGES, ETC.)

ARRABBIATA SAUCE 131
AVOCADO SALSA 131
BUTTERSCOTCH SAUCE 132
CANDIED CITRUS PEEL 133
CANDIED CUCUMBER RINGS
  OR STICKS 134
CINNAMON PECANS 134
CRISP SWEET CUCUMBER
  PICKLES 135
ESSENSEPAULA'S SOFT
  SPIRIT FRUIT WINE 135
HOT MULLED CRANBERRY
  CIDER 135
MARIAN'S SALAD DRESSING 136
MARINATED OLIVES 136
MILLION ISLAND DRESSING 137
ORANGE JULIUS 137
PARTY PUNCH 137
PARTY PUNCH-VARIATION 2 138
PUMPKIN DIP 138
SESAME SAUCE 138
SUMMER SLUSH RECIPE 139
TOMATO GRAVY 139

EATING WELL THROUGH CANCER

APPLE AND PRUNE SAUCE 141
BANANA OAT SHAKE 141
BEAN SOUP 142
COFFEE MILK SHAKE 142

PANTRY BASICS

A WELL-STOCKED PANTRY provides all the makings for a good meal. With the right ingredients, you can quickly create a variety of satisfying, delicious meals for family or guests. Keeping these items in stock also means avoiding extra trips to the grocery store, saving you time and money. Although everyone's pantry is different, there are basic items you should always have. Add other items according to your family's needs. For example, while some families consider chips, cereals and snacks as must-haves, others can't be without feta cheese and imported olives. Use these basic pantry suggestions as a handy reference list when creating your grocery list. Don't forget refrigerated items like milk, eggs, cheese and butter.

STAPLES

Baker's chocolate
Baking powder
Baking soda
Barbeque sauce
Bread crumbs (plain or seasoned)
Chocolate chips
Cocoa powder
Cornmeal
Cornstarch
Crackers
Flour
Honey
Ketchup
Lemon juice
Mayonnaise or salad dressing
Non-stick cooking spray
Nuts (almonds, pecans, walnuts)
Oatmeal
Oil (olive, vegetable)
Pancake baking mix
Pancake syrup
Peanut butter
Shortening
Sugar (granulated, brown, powdered)
Vinegar

PACKAGED/CANNED FOODS

Beans (canned, dry)
Broth (beef, chicken)
Cake mixes with frosting
Canned diced tomatoes
Canned fruit
Canned mushrooms
Canned soup
Canned tomato paste & sauce
Canned tuna & chicken
Cereal
Dried soup mix
Gelatin (flavored or plain)
Gravies
Jarred Salsa
Milk (evaporated, sweetened condensed)
Non-fat dry milk
Pastas
Rice (brown, white)
Spaghetti sauce

SPICES/SEASONINGS

Basil
Bay leaves
Black pepper
Bouillon cubes (beef, chicken)
Chives
Chili powder
Cinnamon
Mustard (dried, prepared)
Garlic powder or salt
Ginger
Nutmeg
Onion powder or salt
Oregano
Paprika
Parsley
Rosemary
Sage
Salt
Soy sauce
Tarragon
Thyme
Vanilla
Worcestershire sauce
Yeast

HERBS & SPICES

DRIED VS. FRESH. While dried herbs are convenient, they don't generally have the same purity of flavor as fresh herbs. Ensure dried herbs are still fresh by checking if they are green and not faded. Crush a few leaves to see if the aroma is still strong. Always store them in an air-tight container away from light and heat.

BASIL
Sweet, warm flavor with an aromatic odor. Use whole or ground. Good with lamb, fish, roast, stews, beef, vegetables, dressing and omelets.

BAY LEAVES
Pungent flavor. Use whole leaf but remove before serving. Good in vegetable dishes, seafood, stews and pickles.

CARAWAY
Spicy taste and aromatic smell. Use in cakes, breads, soups, cheese and sauerkraut.

CELERY SEED
Strong taste which resembles the vegetable. Can be used sparingly in pickles and chutney, meat and fish dishes, salads, bread, marinades, dressings and dips.

CHIVES
Sweet, mild flavor like that of onion. Excellent in salads, fish, soups and potatoes.

CILANTRO
Use fresh. Excellent in salads, fish, chicken, rice, beans and Mexican dishes.

CINNAMON
Sweet, pungent flavor. Widely used in many sweet baked goods, chocolate dishes, cheesecakes, pickles, chutneys and hot drinks.

CORIANDER
Mild, sweet, orangy flavor and available whole or ground. Common in curry powders and pickling spice and also used in chutney, meat dishes, casseroles, Greek-style dishes, apple pies and baked goods.

CURRY POWDER
Spices are combined to proper proportions to give a distinct flavor to meat, poultry, fish and vegetables.

DILL
Both seeds and leaves are flavorful. Leaves may be used as a garnish or cooked with fish, soup, dressings, potatoes and beans. Leaves or the whole plant may be used to flavor pickles.

FENNEL
Sweet, hot flavor. Both seeds and leaves are used. Use in small quantities in pies and baked goods. Leaves can be boiled with fish.

HERBS & SPICES

GINGER
A pungent root, this aromatic spice is sold fresh, dried or ground. Use in pickles, preserves, cakes, cookies, soups and meat dishes.

MARJORAM
May be used both dried or green. Use to flavor fish, poultry, omelets, lamb, stew, stuffing and tomato juice.

MINT
Aromatic with a cool flavor. Excellent in beverages, fish, lamb, cheese, soup, peas, carrots and fruit desserts.

NUTMEG
Whole or ground. Used in chicken and cream soups, cheese dishes, fish cakes, and with chicken and veal. Excellent in custards, milk puddings, pies and cakes.

OREGANO
Strong, aromatic odor. Use whole or ground in tomato juice, fish, eggs, pizza, omelets, chili, stew, gravy, poultry and vegetables.

PAPRIKA
A bright red pepper, this spice is used in meat, vegetables and soups or as a garnish for potatoes, salads or eggs.

PARSLEY
Best when used fresh, but can be used dried as a garnish or as a seasoning. Try in fish, omelets, soup, meat, stuffing and mixed greens.

ROSEMARY
Very aromatic. Can be used fresh or dried. Season fish, stuffing, beef, lamb, poultry, onions, eggs, bread and potatoes. Great in dressings.

SAFFRON
Aromatic, slightly bitter taste. Only a pinch needed to flavor and color dishes such as bouillabaisse, chicken soup, rice, paella, fish sauces, buns and cakes. Very expensive, so where a touch of color is needed, use turmeric instead, but the flavor will not be the same.

SAGE
Use fresh or dried. The flowers are sometimes used in salads. May be used in tomato juice, fish, omelets, beef, poultry, stuffing, cheese spreads and breads.

TARRAGON
Leaves have a pungent, hot taste. Use to flavor sauces, salads, fish, poultry, tomatoes, eggs, green beans, carrots and dressings.

THYME
Sprinkle leaves on fish or poultry before broiling or baking. Throw a few sprigs directly on coals shortly before meat is finished grilling.

TURMERIC
Aromatic, slightly bitter flavor. Should be used sparingly in curry powder and relishes and to color cakes and rice dishes.

Use 3 times more fresh herbs if substituting fresh for dried.

BAKING BREADS

HINTS FOR BAKING BREADS

- Kneading dough for 30 seconds after mixing improves the texture of baking powder biscuits.

- Instead of shortening, use cooking or salad oil in waffles and hot cakes.

- When bread is baking, a small dish of water in the oven will help keep the crust from hardening.

- Dip a spoon in hot water to measure shortening, butter, etc., and the fat will slip out more easily.

- Small amounts of leftover corn may be added to pancake batter for variety.

- To make bread crumbs, use the fine cutter of a food grinder and tie a large paper bag over the spout in order to prevent flying crumbs.

- When you are doing any sort of baking, you get better results if you remember to preheat your cookie sheet, muffin tins or cake pans.

3 RULES FOR USE OF LEAVENING AGENTS

1. In simple flour mixtures, use 2 teaspoons baking powder to leaven 1 cup flour. Reduce this amount 1/2 teaspoon for each egg used.

2. To 1 teaspoon soda, use 2 1/4 teaspoons cream of tartar, 2 cups freshly soured milk or 1 cup molasses.

3. To substitute soda and an acid for baking powder, divide the amount of baking powder by 4. Take that as your measure and add acid according to rule 2.

PROPORTIONS OF BAKING POWDER TO FLOUR

biscuits ....to 1 cup flour use 1 1/4 tsp. baking powder
cake with oil ....to 1 cup flour use 1 tsp. baking powder
muffins ....to 1 cup flour use 1 1/2 tsp. baking powder
popovers ....to 1 cup flour use 1 1/4 tsp. baking powder
waffles ....to 1 cup flour use 1 1/4 tsp. baking powder

PROPORTIONS OF LIQUID TO FLOUR

pour batter ....to 1 cup liquid use 1 cup flour
drop batter ....to 1 cup liquid use 2 to 2 1/2 cups flour
soft dough ....to 1 cup liquid use 3 to 3 1/2 cups flour
stiff dough ....to 1 cup liquid use 4 cups flour

TIME & TEMPERATURE CHART

Breads	Minutes	Temperature
biscuits	12 - 15	400° - 450°
cornbread	25 - 30	400° - 425°
gingerbread	40 - 50	350° - 370°
loaf	50 - 60	350° - 400°
nut bread	50 - 75	350°
popovers	30 - 40	425° - 450°
rolls	20 - 30	400° - 450°

BAKING DESSERTS

PERFECT COOKIES

Cookie dough that must be rolled is much easier to handle after it has been refrigerated for 10 to 30 minutes. This keeps the dough from sticking, even though it may be soft. If not done, the soft dough may require more flour and too much flour makes cookies hard and brittle. Place on a floured board only as much dough as can be easily managed. Flour the rolling pin slightly and roll lightly to desired thickness. Cut shapes close together and add trimmings to dough that needs to be rolled. Place pans or sheets in upper third of oven. Watch cookies carefully while baking in order to avoid burned edges. When sprinkling sugar on cookies, try putting it into a salt shaker in order to save time.

PERFECT PIES

- Pie crust will be better and easier to make if all the ingredients are cool.

- The lower crust should be placed in the pan so that it covers the surface smoothly. Air pockets beneath the surface will push the crust out of shape while baking.

- Folding the top crust over the lower crust before crimping will keep juices in the pie.

- When making custard pie, bake at a high temperature for about 10 minutes to prevent a soggy crust. Then finish baking at a low temperature.

- When making cream pie, sprinkle crust with powdered sugar in order to prevent it from becoming soggy.

PERFECT CAKES

- Fill cake pans two-thirds full and spread batter into corners and sides, leaving a slight hollow in the center.

- Cake is done when it shrinks from the sides of the pan or if it springs back when touched lightly with the finger.

- After removing a cake from the oven, place it on a rack for about 5 minutes. Then, the sides should be loosened and the cake turned out on a rack in order to finish cooling.

- Do not frost cakes until thoroughly cool.

- Icing will remain where you put it if you sprinkle cake with powdered sugar first.

TIME & TEMPERATURE CHART

Dessert	Time	Temperature
butter cake, layer	20-40 min.	380° - 400°
butter cake, loaf	40-60 min.	360° - 400°
cake, angel	50-60 min.	300° - 360°
cake, fruit	3-4 hrs.	275° - 325°
cake, sponge	40-60 min.	300° - 350°
cookies, molasses	18-20 min.	350° - 375°
cookies, thin	10-12 min.	380° - 390°
cream puffs	45-60 min.	300° - 350°
meringue	40-60 min.	250° - 300°
pie crust	20-40 min.	400° - 500°

VEGETABLES FRUITS

COOKING TIME TABLE

Vegetable	Cooking Method	Time
artichokes	boiled	40 min.
	steamed	45-60 min.
asparagus tips	boiled	10-15 min.
beans, lima	boiled	20-40 min.
	steamed	60 min.
beans, string	boiled	15-35 min.
	steamed	60 min.
beets, old	boiled or steamed	1-2 hours.
beets, young with skin	boiled	30 min.
	steamed	60 min.
	baked	70-90 min.
broccoli, flowerets	boiled	5-10 min.
broccoli, stems	boiled	20-30 min.
brussels sprouts	boiled	20-30 min.
cabbage, chopped	boiled	10-20 min.
	steamed	25 min.
carrots, cut across	boiled	8-10 min.
	steamed	40 min.
cauliflower, flowerets	boiled	8-10 min.
cauliflower, stem down	boiled	20-30 min.
corn, green, tender	boiled	5-10 min.
	steamed	15 min.
	baked	20 min.
corn on the cob	boiled	8-10 min.
	steamed	15 min.
eggplant, whole	boiled	30 min.
	steamed	40 min.
	baked	45 min.
parsnips	boiled	25-40 min.
	steamed	60 min.
	baked	60-75 min.
peas, green	boiled or steamed	5-15 min.
potatoes	boiled	20-40 min.
	steamed	60 min.
	baked	45-60 min.
pumpkin or squash	boiled	20-40 min.
	steamed	45 min.
	baked	60 min.
tomatoes	boiled	5-15 min.
turnips	boiled	25-40 min.

DRYING TIME TABLE

Fruit	Sugar or Honey	Cooking Time
apricots	¼ c. for each cup of fruit	about 40 min.
figs	1 T. for each cup of fruit	about 30 min.
peaches	¼ c. for each cup of fruit	about 45 min.
prunes	2 T. for each cup of fruit	about 45 min.

VEGETABLES & FRUITS

BUYING FRESH VEGETABLES

Artichokes: Look for compact, tightly closed heads with green, clean-looking leaves. Avoid those with leaves that are brown or separated.

Asparagus: Stalks should be tender and firm; tips should be close and compact. Choose the stalks with very little white; they are more tender. Use asparagus soon because it toughens quickly.

Beans, Snap: Those with small seeds inside the pods are best. Avoid beans with dry-looking pods.

Broccoli, Brussels Sprouts and Cauliflower: Flower clusters on broccoli and cauliflower should be tight and close together. Brussels sprouts should be firm and compact. Smudgy, dirty spots may indicate pests or disease.

Cabbage and Head Lettuce: Choose heads that are heavy for their size. Avoid cabbage with worm holes and lettuce with discoloration or soft rot.

Cucumbers: Choose long, slender cucumbers for best quality. May be dark or medium green, but yellow ones are undesirable.

Mushrooms: Caps should be closed around the stems. Avoid black or brown gills.

Peas and Lima Beans: Select pods that are well-filled but not bulging. Avoid dried, spotted, yellow or limp pods.

BUYING FRESH FRUITS

Bananas: Skin should be free of bruises and black or brown spots. Purchase them slightly green and allow them to ripen at room temperature.

Berries: Select plump, solid berries with good color. Avoid stained containers which indicate wet or leaky berries. Berries with clinging caps, such as blackberries and raspberries, may be unripe. Strawberries without caps may be overripe.

Melons: In cantaloupes, thick, close netting on the rind indicates best quality. Cantaloupes are ripe when the stem scar is smooth and the space between the netting is yellow or yellow-green. They are best when fully ripe with fruity odor.

Honeydews are ripe when rind has creamy to yellowish color and velvety texture. Immature honeydews are whitish-green.

Ripe watermelons have some yellow color on one side. If melons are white or pale green on one side, they are not ripe.

Oranges, Grapefruit and Lemons: Choose those heavy for their size. Smoother, thinner skins usually indicate more juice. Most skin markings do not affect quality. Oranges with a slight greenish tinge may be just as ripe as fully colored ones. Light or greenish-yellow lemons are more tart than deep yellow ones. Avoid citrus fruits showing withered, sunken or soft areas.

NAPKIN FOLDING

FOR BEST RESULTS, use well-starched linen napkins if possible. For more complicated folds, 24-inch napkins work best. Practice the folds with newspapers. Children will have fun decorating the table once they learn these attractive folds!

SHIELD

Easy fold. Elegant with monogram in corner.

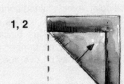

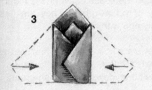

Instructions:
1. Fold into quarter size. If monogrammed, ornate corner should face down.
2. Turn up folded corner three-quarters.
3. Overlap right side and left side points.
4. Turn over; adjust sides so they are even, single point in center.
5. Place point up or down on plate, or left of plate.

ROSETTE

Elegant on plate.

Instructions:
1. Fold left and right edges to center, leaving 1/2" opening along center.
2. Pleat firmly from top edge to bottom edge. Sharpen edges with hot iron.
3. Pinch center together. If necessary, use small piece of pipe cleaner to secure and top with single flower.
4. Spread out rosette.

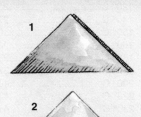

CANDLE

Easy to do; can be decorated.

Instructions:
1. Fold into triangle, point at top.
2. Turn lower edge up 1".
3. Turn over, folded edge down.
4. Roll tightly from left to right.
5. Tuck in corner. Stand upright.

FAN

Pretty in napkin ring or on plate.

Instructions:
1. Fold top and bottom edges to center.
2. Fold top and bottom edges to center a second time.
3. Pleat firmly from the left edge. Sharpen edges with hot iron.
4. Spread out fan. Balance flat folds of each side on table. Well-starched napkins will hold shape.

LILY

Effective and pretty on table.

Instructions:
1. Fold napkin into quarters.
2. Fold into triangle, closed corner to open points.
3. Turn two points over to other side. (Two points are on either side of closed point.)
4. Pleat.
5. Place closed end in glass. Pull down two points on each side and shape.

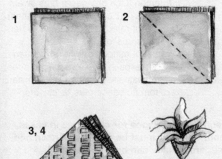

MEASUREMENTS & SUBSTITUTIONS

MEASUREMENTS

a pinch	1/8 teaspoon or less
3 teaspoons	1 tablespoon
4 tablespoons	1/4 cup
8 tablespoons	1/2 cup
12 tablespoons	3/4 cup
16 tablespoons	1 cup
2 cups	1 pint
4 cups	1 quart
4 quarts	1 gallon
8 quarts	1 peck
4 pecks	1 bushel
16 ounces	1 pound
32 ounces	1 quart
1 ounce liquid	2 tablespoons
8 ounces liquid	1 cup

Use standard measuring spoons and cups. All measurements are level.

C° TO F° CONVERSION

120° C	250° F
140° C	275° F
150° C	300° F
160° C	325° F
180° C	350° F
190° C	375° F
200° C	400° F
220° C	425° F
230° C	450° F

Temperature conversions are estimates.

SUBSTITUTIONS

Ingredient	Quantity	Substitute
baking powder	1 teaspoon	1/4 tsp. baking soda plus 1/2 tsp. cream of tartar
chocolate	1 square (1 oz.)	3 or 4 T. cocoa plus 1 T. butter
cornstarch	1 tablespoon	2 T. flour or 2 tsp. quick-cooking tapioca
cracker crumbs	3/4 cup	1 c. bread crumbs
dates	1 lb.	1 1/2 c. dates, pitted and cut
dry mustard	1 teaspoon	1 T. prepared mustard
flour, self-rising	1 cup	1 c. all-purpose flour, 1/2 tsp. salt, and 1 tsp. baking powder
herbs, fresh	1 tablespoon	1 tsp. dried herbs
ketchup or chili sauce	1 cup	1 c. tomato sauce plus 1/2 c. sugar and 2 T. vinegar (for use in cooking)
milk, sour	1 cup	1 T. lemon juice or vinegar plus sweet milk to make 1 c. (let stand 5 minutes)
whole	1 cup	1/2 c. evaporated milk plus 1/2 c. water
min. marshmallows	10	1 lg. marshmallow
onion, fresh	1 small	1 T. instant minced onion, rehydrated
sugar, brown	1/2 cup	2 T. molasses in 1/2 c. granulated sugar
powdered	1 cup	1 c. granulated sugar plus 1 tsp. cornstarch
tomato juice	1 cup	1/2 c. tomato sauce plus 1/2 c. water

When substituting cocoa for chocolate in cakes, the amount of flour must be reduced. Brown and white sugars usually can be interchanged.

SUGAR

EQUIVALENCY CHART

Food	Quantity	Yield
apple	1 medium	1 cup
banana, mashed	1 medium	1/3 cup
bread	1 1/2 slices	1 cup soft crumbs
bread	1 slice	1/4 cup fine, dry crumbs
butter	1 stick or 1/4 pound	1/2 cup
cheese, American, cubed	1 pound	2 2/3 cups
American, grated	1 pound	5 cups
cream cheese	3-ounce package	6 2/3 tablespoons
chocolate, bitter	1 square	1 ounce
cocoa	1 pound	4 cups
coconut	1 1/2 pound package	2 2/3 cups
coffee, ground	1 pound	5 cups
cornmeal	1 pound	3 cups
cornstarch	1 pound	3 cups
crackers, graham	14 squares	1 cup fine crumbs
saltine	28 crackers	1 cup fine crumbs
egg	4-5 whole	1 cup
whites	8-10	1 cup
yolks	10-12	1 cup
evaporated milk	1 cup	3 cups whipped
flour, cake, sifted	1 pound	4 1/2 cups
rye	1 pound	5 cups
white, sifted	1 pound	4 cups
white, unsifted	1 pound	3 3/4 cups
gelatin, flavored	3 1/4 ounces	1/2 cup
unflavored	1/4 ounce	1 tablespoon
lemon	1 medium	3 tablespoon juice
marshmallows	16	1/4 pound
noodles, cooked	8-ounce package	7 cups
uncooked	4 ounces (1 1/2 cups)	2-3 cups cooked
macaroni, cooked	8-ounce package	6 cups
macaroni, uncooked	4 ounces (1 1/4 cups)	2 1/4 cups cooked
spaghetti, uncooked	7 ounces	4 cups cooked
nuts, chopped	1/4 pound	1 cup
almonds	1 pound	3 1/2 cups
walnuts, broken	1 pound	3 cups
walnuts, unshelled	1 pound	1 1/2 to 1 3/4 cups
onion	1 medium	1/2 cup
orange	3-4 medium	1 cup juice
raisins	1 pound	3 1/2 cups
rice, brown	1 cup	4 cups cooked
converted	1 cup	3 1/2 cups cooked
regular	1 cup	3 cups cooked
wild	1 cup	4 cups cooked
sugar, brown	1 pound	2 1/2 cups
powdered	1 pound	3 1/2 cups
white	1 pound	2 cups
vanilla wafers	22	1 cup fine crumbs
zwieback, crumbled	4	1 cups

FOOD QUANTITIES

FOR LARGE SERVINGS

	25 Servings	50 Servings	100 Servings
Beverages:			
coffee	½ pound and 1½ gallons water	1 pound and 3 gallons water	2 pounds and 6 gallons water
lemonade	10-15 lemons and 1½ gallons water	20-30 lemons and 3 gallons water	40-60 lemons and 6 gallons water
tea	1/12 pound and 1½ gallons water	⅙ pound and 3 gallons water	⅓ pound and 6 gallons water
Desserts:			
layered cake	1 12" cake	3 10" cakes	6 10" cakes
sheet cake	1 10" x 12" cake	1 12" x 20" cake	2 12" x 20" cakes
watermelon	37 ½ pounds	75 pounds	150 pounds
whipping cream	¾ pint	1½ to 2 pints	3-4 pints
Ice cream:			
brick	3 ¼ quarts	6 ½ quarts	13 quarts
bulk	2 ¼ quarts	4 ½ quarts or 1 ¼ gallons	9 quarts or 2 ½ gallons
Meat, poultry or fish:			
fish	13 pounds	25 pounds	50 pounds
fish, fillets or steak	7 ½ pounds	15 pounds	30 pounds
hamburger	9 pounds	18 pounds	35 pounds
turkey or chicken	13 pounds	25 to 35 pounds	50 to 75 pounds
wieners (beef)	6 ½ pounds	13 pounds	25 pounds
Salads, casseroles:			
baked beans	¾ gallon	1 ¼ gallons	2 ½ gallons
jello salad	¾ gallon	1 ¼ gallons	2 ½ gallons
potato salad	4 ¼ quarts	2 ¼ gallons	4 ½ gallons
scalloped potatoes	4 ½ quarts or 1 12" x 20" pan	9 quarts or 2 ¼ gallons	18 quarts 4 ½ gallons
spaghetti	1 ¼ gallons	2 ½ gallons	5 gallons
Sandwiches:			
bread	50 slices or 3 1-pound loaves	100 slices or 6 1-pound loaves	200 slices or 12 1-pound loaves
butter	½ pound	1 pound	2 pounds
lettuce	1 ½ heads	3 heads	6 heads
mayonnaise	1 cup	2 cups	4 cups
mixed filling			
meat, eggs, fish	1 ½ quarts	3 quarts	6 quarts
jam, jelly	1 quart	2 quarts	4 quarts

PRACTICALLY EVERYONE has experienced that dreadful moment in the kitchen when a recipe failed and dinner guests have arrived. Perhaps a failed timer, distraction or a missing or mismeasured ingredient is to blame. These handy tips can save the day!

Acidic foods – Sometimes a tomato-based sauce will become too acidic. Add baking soda, one teaspoon at a time, to the sauce. Use sugar as a sweeter alternative.

Burnt food on pots and pans – Allow the pan to cool on its own. Remove as much of the food as possible. Fill with hot water and add a capful of liquid fabric softener to the pot; let it stand for a few hours. You'll have an easier time removing the burnt food.

Chocolate seizes – Chocolate can seize (turn course and grainy) when it comes into contact with water. Place seized chocolate in a metal bowl over a large saucepan with an inch of simmering water in it. Over medium heat, slowly whisk in warm heavy cream. Use 1/4 cup cream to 4 ounces of chocolate. The chocolate will melt and become smooth.

Forgot to thaw whipped topping – Thaw in microwave for 1 minute on the defrost setting. Stir to blend well. Do not over thaw!

Hands smell like garlic or onion – Rinse hands under cold water while rubbing them with a large stainless steel spoon.

Hard brown sugar – Place in a paper bag and microwave for a few seconds, or place hard chunks in a food processor.

Jello too hard – Heat on a low microwave power setting for a very short time.

Lumpy gravy or sauce – Use a blender, food processor or simply strain.

No tomato juice – Mix 1/2 cup ketchup with 1/2 cup water.

Out of honey – Substitute 1 1/4 cups sugar dissolved in 1 cup water.

Overcooked sweet potatoes or carrots – Softened sweet potatoes and carrots make a wonderful soufflé with the addition of eggs and sugar. Consult your favorite cookbook for a good soufflé recipe. Overcooked sweet potatoes can also be used as pie filling.

Sandwich bread is stale – Toast or microwave bread briefly. Otherwise, turn it into breadcrumbs. Bread exposed to light and heat will hasten its demise, so consider using a bread box.

Soup, sauce, gravy too thin – Add 1 tablespoon of flour to hot soup, sauce or gravy. Whisk well (to avoid lumps) while the mixture is boiling. Repeat if necessary.

Sticky rice – Rinse rice with warm water.

Stew or soup is greasy – Refrigerate and remove grease once it congeals. Another trick is to lay cold lettuce leaves over the hot stew for about 10 seconds and then remove. Repeat as necessary.

Too salty – Add a little sugar and vinegar. For soups or sauces, add a raw peeled potato.

Too sweet – Add a little vinegar or lemon juice.

Undercooked cakes and cookies – Serve over vanilla ice cream. You can also layer pieces of cake or cookies with whipped cream and fresh fruit to form a dessert parfait. Crumbled cookies also make an excellent ice cream or cream pie topping.

COUNTING CALORIES

BEVERAGES

apple juice, 6 oz.	90
coffee (black)	0
cola, 12 oz.	115
cranberry juice, 6 oz.	115
ginger ale, 12 oz.	115
grape juice, (prepared from frozen concentrate), 6 oz.	142
lemonade, (prepared from frozen concentrate), 6 oz.	85
milk, protein fortified, 1 c.	105
skim, 1 c.	90
whole, 1 c.	160
orange juice, 6 oz.	85
pineapple juice, unsweetened, 6 oz.	95
root beer, 12 oz.	150
tonic (quinine water) 12 oz.	132

BREADS

cornbread, 1 sm. square	130
dumplings, 1 med.	70
French toast, 1 slice	135
melba toast, 1 slice	25
muffins, blueberry, 1 muffin	110
bran, 1 muffin	106
corn, 1 muffin	125
English, 1 muffin	280
pancakes, 1 (4-in.)	60
pumpernickel, 1 slice	75
rye, 1 slice	60
waffle, 1	216
white, 1 slice	60-70
whole wheat, 1 slice	55-65

CEREALS

cornflakes, 1 c.	105
cream of wheat, 1 c.	120
oatmeal, 1 c.	148
rice flakes, 1 c.	105
shredded wheat, 1 biscuit	100
sugar krisps, 3/4 c.	110

CRACKERS

graham, 1 cracker	15-30
rye crisp, 1 cracker	35
saltine, 1 cracker	17-20
wheat thins, 1 cracker	9

DAIRY PRODUCTS

butter or margarine, 1 T.	100
cheese, American, 1 oz.	100
camembert, 1 oz.	85
cheddar, 1 oz.	115
cottage cheese, 1 oz.	30
mozzarella, 1 oz.	90
parmesan, 1 oz.	130
ricotta, 1 oz.	50
roquefort, 1 oz.	105
Swiss, 1 oz.	105
cream, light, 1 T.	30
heavy, 1 T.	55
sour, 1 T.	45
hot chocolate, with milk, 1 c.	277
milk chocolate, 1 oz.	145-155
yogurt	
made w/ whole milk, 1 c.	150-165
made w/ skimmed milk, 1 c.	125

EGGS

fried, 1 lg.	100
poached or boiled, 1 lg.	75-80
scrambled or in omelet, 1 lg.	110-130

FISH AND SEAFOOD

bass, 4 oz.	105
salmon, broiled or baked, 3 oz.	155
sardines, canned in oil, 3 oz.	170
trout, fried, 3 1/2 oz.	220
tuna, in oil, 3 oz.	170
in water, 3 oz.	110

COUNTING CALORIES

FRUITS

apple, 1 med. 80-100
applesauce, sweetened, ½ c. 90-115
   unsweetened, ½ c. 50
banana, 1 med. 85
blueberries, ½ c. 45
cantaloupe, ½ c. 24
cherries (pitted), raw, ½ c. 40
grapefruit, ½ med. 55
grapes, ½ c. 35-55
honeydew, ½ c. 55
mango, 1 med. 90
orange, 1 med. 65-75
peach, 1 med. 35
pear, 1 med. 60-100
pineapple, fresh, ½ c. 40
   canned in syrup, ½ c. 95
plum, 1 med. 30
strawberries, fresh, ½ c. 30
   frozen and sweetened, ½ c. ..120-140
tangerine, 1 lg. 39
watermelon, ½ c. 42

MEAT AND POULTRY

beef, ground (lean), 3 oz. 185
   roast, 3 oz. 185
chicken, broiled, 3 oz. 115
lamb chop (lean), 3 oz. 175-200
steak, sirloin, 3 oz. 175
   tenderloin, 3 oz. 174
   top round, 3 oz. 162
turkey, dark meat, 3 oz. 175
   white meat, 3 oz. 150
veal, cutlet, 3 oz. 156
   roast, 3 oz. 76

NUTS

almonds, 2 T. 105
cashews, 2 T. 100
peanuts, 2 T. 105
peanut butter, 1 T. 95
pecans, 2 T. 95
pistachios, 2 T. 92
walnuts, 2 T. 80

PASTA

macaroni or spaghetti,
   cooked, ¾ c. 115

SALAD DRESSINGS

blue cheese, 1 T. 70
French, 1 T. 65
Italian, 1 T. 80
mayonnaise, 1 T. 100
olive oil, 1 T. 124
Russian, 1 T. 70
salad oil, 1 T. 120

SOUPS

bean, 1 c. 130-180
beef noodle, 1 c. 70
bouillon and consomme, 1 c. 30
chicken noodle, 1 c. 65
chicken with rice, 1 c. 50
minestrone, 1 c. 80-150
split pea, 1 c. 145-170
tomato with milk, 1 c. 170
vegetable, 1 c. 80-100

VEGETABLES

asparagus, 1 c. 35
broccoli, cooked, ½ c. 25
cabbage, cooked, ½ c. 15-20
carrots, cooked, ½ c. 25-30
cauliflower, ½ c. 10-15
corn (kernels), ½ c. 70
green beans, 1 c. 30
lettuce, shredded, ½ c. 5
mushrooms, canned, ½ c. 20
onions, cooked, ½ c. 30
peas, cooked, ½ c. 60
potato, baked, 1 med. 90
   chips, 8-10 100
   mashed, w/milk & butter, 1 c. ..200-300
spinach, 1 c. 40
tomato, raw, 1 med. 25
   cooked, ½ c. 30

COOKING TERMS

Au gratin: Topped with crumbs and/or cheese and browned in oven or under broiler.

Au jus: Served in its own juices.

Baste: To moisten foods during cooking with pan drippings or special sauce in order to add flavor and prevent drying.

Bisque: A thick cream soup.

Blanch: To immerse in rapidly boiling water and allow to cook slightly.

Cream: To soften a fat, especially butter, by beating it at room temperature. Butter and sugar are often creamed together, making a smooth, soft paste.

Crimp: To seal the edges of a two-crust pie either by pinching them at intervals with the fingers or by pressing them together with the tines of a fork.

Crudites: An assortment of raw vegetables (i.e. carrots, broccoli, celery, mushrooms) that is served as an hors d'oeuvre, often accompanied by a dip.

Degrease: To remove fat from the surface of stews, soups or stock. Usually cooled in the refrigerator so that fat hardens and is easily removed.

Dredge: To coat lightly with flour, corn-meal, etc.

Entree: The main course.

Fold: To incorporate a delicate substance, such as whipped cream or beaten egg whites, into another substance without releasing air bubbles. A spatula is used to gently bring part of the mixture from the bottom of the bowl to the top. The process is repeated, while slowly rotating the bowl, until the ingredients are thoroughly blended.

Glaze: To cover with a glossy coating, such as a melted and somewhat diluted jelly for fruit desserts.

Julienne: To cut or slice vegetables, fruits or cheeses into match-shaped slivers.

Marinate: To allow food to stand in a liquid in order to tenderize or to add flavor.

Meuniére: Dredged with flour and sautéed in butter.

Mince: To chop food into very small pieces.

Parboil: To boil until partially cooked; to blanch. Usually final cooking in a seasoned sauce follows this procedure.

Pare: To remove the outermost skin of a fruit or vegetable.

Poach: To cook gently in hot liquid kept just below the boiling point.

Purée: To mash foods by hand by rubbing through a sieve or food mill, or by whirling in a blender or food processor until perfectly smooth.

Refresh: To run cold water over food that has been parboiled in order to stop the cooking process quickly.

Sauté: To cook and/or brown food in a small quantity of hot shortening.

Scald: To heat to just below the boiling point, when tiny bubbles appear at the edge of the saucepan.

Simmer: To cook in liquid just below the boiling point. The surface of the liquid should be barely moving, broken from time to time by slowly rising bubbles.

Steep: To let food stand in hot liquid in order to extract or to enhance flavor, like tea in hot water or poached fruit in syrup.

Toss: To combine ingredients with a repeated lifting motion.

Whip: To beat rapidly in order to incorporate air and produce expansion, as in heavy cream or egg whites.

You supply the recipes and we'll do the rest!™

Publish Your Own Cookbook

Churches, schools, organizations, and families can preserve their favorite recipes by publishing a custom cookbook. Cookbooks make a great **fundraiser** because they are easy to sell and highly profitable. Our low prices make cookbooks the perfect affordable **keepsake**. Morris Press Cookbooks is the nation's leading publisher of community cookbooks. We offer:

- Low prices, high quality, and prompt service.
- Many options and styles to suit your needs.
- 90 days to pay and a written no-risk guarantee.

Order our FREE Cookbook Kit for all the details:

- Call us at **800-445-6621, ext. CB**
- Visit our web site at **www.morriscookbooks.com**
- Mail the **postage-paid reply card** below.

Discover the right ingredients for a really great cookbook.

Order our **FREE** Cookbook Kit. Please print neatly.

Name_____

Organization _____

Address _____

City _____ State _____ Zip_____

Email _____

Phone (_____)_____

Back Card 6-06

MORRIS PRESS
COOKBOOKS

P. O. Box 2110 • Kearney, NE 68848

Morris Press Cookbooks has all the right ingredients to make a really great cookbook. Your group can raise $500–$50,000 or create a cookbook as a lasting keepsake, preserving favorite family recipes.

3 ways to order our **FREE** Cookbook Kit:
- Call us at **800-445-6621, ext. CB**.
- Visit our web site at **www.morriscookbooks.com**.
- Complete and mail the **postage-paid reply card** below.